Lay Speaking Ministries:

Basic Course
2005–2006

John P. Gilbert
Nancy C. Zoller

DISCIPLESHIP RESOURCES

PO BOX 340003 • NASHVILLE, TN 37203-0003

www.discipleshipresources.org

ISBN 0-88177-454-5

DR454

CONTENTS

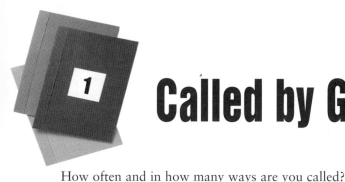

Called by God

How often and in how many ways are you called?

You may be accustomed to being called by your first name by friends and the people you see every day. Business associates may call you by your last name, preceded by a courtesy title such as Miss, Mr., Mrs., or Ms. In your professional life, you may be called Doctor, Your Honor, or Professor. If you are a parent, you may be called Dad or Mom. Grandchildren may call you Grandma, Gramps, Nana, or Poppa.

Does a parent have a special name for you? Remember when your mother or father wanted something important? They often called you by your first, middle, and last name—emphatically!

What about your spouse? Does your spouse have a pet name for you: Hon, Dear, or some other special name that has meaning just for the two of you?

Write down how many times you are called during a day—include those annoying dinnertime telemarketing calls.

Most of us go through each day being called so many times that we become deaf to The Call.

This call is God's call to us, for us, on us. It is the summons of God to respond to God's call to serve, to minister, to celebrate, to sacrifice, to answer. God's call is not a one-time event. It is not a single cataclysmic summons, although it can be that. No, God's call is a repeated and repeating summons, one that resounds through every moment of our lives. God has made us to be in fellowship and service to and with God; God never ceases to summon us to fulfill the ministry to which we are called.

Perhaps most significantly, God calls us by our own given name. God knows each of us as intimately as our spouses, parents, children, and friends know us. Read Isaiah 43:1. God says to each of us, "I have called you by name, you are mine."

Do you doubt whether you have been called by God? Be attentive. Discerning God's call is not always an easy task, especially among the distractions of other daily calls.

For example, you are reading this manual because you have felt a call to explore the Lay Speaking Ministries in The United Methodist Church. You may be thinking: *I am reading this because my pastor (Sunday school teacher, spouse, friend, or lay leader) talked me into it. I am not sure I want to be a lay speaker. I am not sure what a lay speaker is! How can that be a call from God?*

Think about the variety of ways God calls us. Who can say that God cannot use a pastor, a Sunday school teacher, a friend who talked you into it? Remember when we suggested earlier that God is calling all of us all of the time? That "all of us" includes you. God is calling you!

Notice the record in the Bible of God working with people throughout the centuries. God called Moses from out of a burning bush. God called Mary in a dream. God called Esther through the frightened words of her cousin Mordecai, "for such a time as this." God called Saul through a blinding light on the road to Damascus. God called Samuel through a voice in the night. God called Martha out of the busyness of the kitchen and into the circle of God's love. God called Gideon repeatedly, despite his protests and demands for proof. God called Sarah when she truly believed she was beyond calling. God called Amos when he was a simple herdsman and dresser of sycamore trees. God called Jeremiah even before he was born. God called Elijah through a still, small voice. God called Peter, James, and John with a quiet "Follow me." God called Matthew from his tax collection table and Zacchaeus out of a tree. God called Abraham in the midst of his success and Jacob in the midst of his failure. God called a Gentile foreigner on the road to Gaza, a harlot at a well in Samaria, a Canaanite woman who dared to argue with Jesus, and a thief hanging on a cross.

Do you need more examples? God called the young man who became Saint Augustine through the songs of children next door. God called Martin Luther through a thunderstorm and John Wesley through the droning voice of a friend who was reading a theological tome aloud. God called literally thousands through the agony of the civil rights and the antiwar movements.

Perhaps it is more accurate to say that each person became aware of God's call in the existing situations and settings. It is not that God had failed to call before; rather, the call had finally become obvious, clear, and compelling.

That is what is happening to you. And that is why you are reading this manual and preparing to become a lay speaker in The United Methodist Church. God's call finally broke through to you. Again, it is not that God fails to call; the problem is that we are not always open to God's call and summons.

If God is calling you (and each of us), then what is the content of that call? What is God calling us to do and to be?

Put most simply, God is calling each of us to be witnesses who proclaim the presence and power of God through all that we are and all that we do. God is calling each of us to tell others about God's love and forgiveness. God is calling us to be God's spokespersons on earth in calling all people into a life-giving and life-sustaining relationship with God through Jesus Christ.

The message may be simple, but the ways we proclaim the message are as varied as the people who hear the call. People hear the call and live it out in an endless variety of ways. You have heard that call (even though you are still discerning it), and one way you want to live it out is through Lay Speaking Ministries. You are responding to a call by God to be a lay speaker. And that call, like the call to any other ministry, must be followed by preparation, practice, and evaluation. That is why you have enrolled in this basic course in lay speaking.

Two warnings: First, each of us responds to God's call out of a sense of humility. God's calls to people are not in any order of importance. Your call to lay speaking sets you apart as a lay speaker. However, it does not confer upon you a status, rank, or privilege that is not shared by every other Christian who responds to God's call, whatever the call may be. Rejoice and celebrate that God has called you to be a lay speaker! But rejoice and celebrate in humility. Brother Lawrence, a monk of the Middle Ages, was called to wash dishes in a monastery kitchen, and he dedicated himself to washing each of those dishes to the glory of God. Self-importance, self-righteousness, or status had no place then, and they have no place today as Christians respond to the call of God to proclaim God's will in the world.

Second, we are imperfect human beings. Our perceptions may not always be completely accurate. Right now you may feel that you are called to Lay Speaking Ministries and may be entering into this wholeheartedly. But you may discover during the course of this study that lay speaking is not for you, that God is calling you to service through some other means. Rejoice in that perception! Do not consider yourself or your response to God's call a failure. Instead, praise God for the insight that helped you discern a more accurate call and enabled you to respond to that call more fully. As authors, we hope that you will discover the fulfillment of God's call to you to be a lay speaker. But should you discern God's will for

you in another direction, we celebrate with you God's call and your response—whatever form it takes!

Before your next session, and even before you read the next chapter in this manual, you need to carry out some activities in preparation for the first session. Choose and complete at least three of these activities, and be ready to share your thoughts with the others in the lay speaking course.

1. Look up the stories of the scriptural figures mentioned earlier in this chapter who felt God's call. Read each one; then determine which of these calls, if any, is most similar to your own sense of call. Write down or tape-record the similarities you see and the reasons for these similarities.

2. Interview a pastor, deacon, Christian educator, or some other person who has chosen full-time Christian service as a profession. Ask questions about that person's sense of call. Was it slow and gradual or sudden and dramatic? What confirmed the sense of call? Has this person ever questioned the call? When and why? Again, write down the thoughts and responses or record them on a tape recorder—with the other person's permission, of course.

3. Recall the two or three people in your life who have had the most impact on your faith as a Christian. Think about their call. What form and shape did that call take? To what were they called? How did their call affect you as you came into contact with them? Again, record your answers on paper or on a tape recorder.

4. Describe in detail your sense of God's call on you and your life. You might do this by writing down your ideas and thoughts in an outline, by recording your ideas and thoughts on a tape recorder, or by symbolically representing your sense of call through a drawing, painting, or some other form of expression. This may be a good time to start keeping a journal or a daily record of your sense of God's call on your life. Record the times and experiences in and through which you feel God's call. Continue to keep this journal even after completing this course.

2 Called to Proclaim the Gospel

Called to proclaim the Word of God!
Yes, but what is the Word of God?
Called to proclaim God's will for the world!
Great! But what is God's will for the world?

Turn on your television and flip to the cable channels. You can almost always find someone promoting his or her perception of the Word of God and God's will for the world. Visit a bookstore to check out the religion section, and you will discover dozens of books, each proclaiming to contain the Word of God and God's will for the world. Visit the worship services of a dozen different denominations and independent churches. In each you will probably hear claims of sole possession of God's truth. The trouble is that these television preachers, authors, denominations, and independent churches do not agree as to what the Word of God is or what God's will for the world is today.

So, what do you as a lay speaker in The United Methodist Church proclaim? What is the Word of God given to you and to those who find a faith home within The United Methodist Church? What do we believe to be God's will and way for the world?

The answer is not as easy to determine as the question is to ask!

Ever since the Resurrection of Christ Jesus that first Easter morning, ever since the apostles first heard the story of the women running back from the now-empty tomb, Christians have been struggling to define just what the Word of God is and what God's will for the world is. Scholars have devoted lifetimes and millions upon millions of words in thousands and thousands of books and articles to answer those questions. The reason answering these questions is so difficult is that God and the ways of God are simply beyond our comprehension and understanding! God is so infinitely greater than we are that we cannot capture and contain God in a single book or article or even in a whole library of books! We cannot understand God completely, for if we could, we could manage or control God, and we certainly know we cannot do that. While the prophecy of Isaiah was dealing with a different set of ideas—and we are taking these verses "out of context"—nonetheless Isaiah 55:8-9 addresses this situation:

For my thoughts are not your thoughts,
	nor are your ways my ways, says the LORD.
For as the heavens are higher than the earth,
	so are my ways higher than your ways
	and my thoughts than your thoughts.

But—and this is an important "but"—this does not excuse us from trying to understand God and the ways of God. This does not excuse us from using all the rational abilities God has given us to describe what we know of God and of God's ways. This does not excuse us from thinking through as carefully as we can all we know and experience of God so that we can communicate that as clearly, as precisely, as comprehensibly as we can to and for others. And when we do that, we are doing the task of theology, for theology is simply thinking about God and stating what we know of God in ways that can be understood and communicated.

We as a United Methodist denomination have struggled with theology, as has every other denomination. Following the lead of the one credited with founding the movement that became our denomination, John Wesley, the eighteenth-century Anglican clergyman, we as a denomination have decided that we will not have a single statement of theology in the form of a confession or creed to which all United Methodists must ascribe. This is not meant to diminish or reject creeds and confessions; indeed, these are signposts that point us toward God, and they are vitally important in our journey of faith. But just as you and I cannot say all there is to be said about God, neither can a single statement, creed, or confession say all there is to be said about God. So we United Methodists use creeds and confessions to help us understand the Word of God and the will of God, but we do not require all people who would join with us to accept without question a creed or confession—nor do we reject from our communion those who might experience discomfort with or even disagree with a single word or sentence in a creed or confession.

So how do we United Methodists do theology? And what are the tools we use to do theology, that is, to think about and to communicate about God?

Through our General Conference, the only group within our denomination that can speak for The United Methodist Church, we United Methodists have developed a way to think theologically and a way to "do" theology, and have presented that way to all United Methodists through a book called *The Book of Discipline of The United Methodist Church.* This book is published every four years (after each General Conference), and much of it is devoted to administrative order and the like.

But a significant part of the *Book of Discipline* is Part II: "Doctrinal Standards and Our Theological Task."

It is the clear responsibility of every lay speaker in The United Methodist Church to have read, re-read, discussed, and prayed about this section of the *Discipline,* for it describes how we as United Methodists believe and, to an extent, what we believe. It also describes some of the background of our beliefs and ways of doing theology and includes a number of important historical documents that illuminate our theology today.

If you have read this far, you may be thinking, "Hold on! What we believe is the Bible! The Bible is the Word of God and tells us the will of God! Right?"

Right. Up to a point. And that point is that everyone uses and misuses the Bible. Just as we took a passage of Isaiah out of context a few paragraphs ago, so do others take statements of the Bible out of context to prove, rationalize, or justify whatever they wish. This example is not intended to diminish the importance of the Bible; but it is meant to emphasize the importance of reading and studying the Bible carefully, entirely, and in the company of other committed Christians. Let us put this another way: John Wesley said in one of those important historical documents that illuminate our theology today that "The Holy Scripture containeth all things necessary to salvation."

So. ... What is it that we United Methodists believe?

Again, the answer is not simple and direct, but the *Book of Discipline* helps us to get a handle on our beliefs. (All quotations in the rest of this chapter are from *The Book of Discipline of the United Methodist Church—2004.* Copyright © 2004 by The United Methodist Publishing House. Used by permission.)

Starting at the beginning of this crucial Part II (¶ 101) is the recognition that we "share a common heritage with Christians of every age and nation." We United Methodists accept, as do most other Christians, several basic understandings about God. These are called Basic Christian Affirmations, and you as a Lay Speaker need to be familiar with these. We can give some of those affirmations in shorthand here, but please read of them completely in the *Discipline.*

"We hold in common with all Christians a faith in the mystery of salvation in and through Jesus Christ." (Note that word *mystery.* We may never understand just how salvation comes about; we only know that it does, for we have experienced it.)

"We share the Christian belief that God's redemptive love is realized in human life by the activity of the Holy Spirit, both in personal experience and in the community of believers." (Do you catch the emphasis on both personal experience and the community of believers? You cannot be a Christian alone!)

"We understand ourselves to be part of Christ's universal church when by adoration, proclamation, and service we become conformed to Christ." (Read between the lines; we United Methodists do not claim to have a corner on truth, nor do we insist that all must be just like us in order to know God's salvation through Christ.)

"With other Christians we recognize that the reign of God is both a present and future reality."

"We share with many Christian communions a recognition of the authority of Scripture in matters of faith, the confession that our justification as sinners is by grace through faith, and the sober realization that the church is in need of continual reformation and renewal."

Thus, in a number of ways, our theology is like that of many other Christian groups. But—there is that word again—but we United Methodists lift up in particular several dimensions of our Christian faith. These are known as the Distinctive Wesleyan Emphases.

Paramount among these emphases (read about all of them in Part II of the *Book of Discipline*) is a focus on the grace of God. "Grace pervades our understanding of Christian faith and life. By grace we mean the undeserved, unmerited, and loving action of God in human existence through the ever-present Holy Spirit." In other words, an individual who did not believe in or accept the grace of God would not be comfortable in a United Methodist congregation.

But we emphasize other things as well, such as:

Prevenient Grace—which is God's "love that surrounds all humanity and precedes any and all of our conscious impulses," and which is one of the many reasons United Methodists practice infant baptism.

Justification and Assurance.

Sanctification and Perfection. Please read about these ideas in the *Book of Discipline.*

Faith and Good Works. Crucial to understanding our United Methodist theology is understanding the relationship between faith and works. To quote the *Discipline*: "We see God's grace and human activity working together in the relationship of faith and good works. God's grace calls forth human response and discipline. Faith is the only response essential for salvation. However, ... salvation evidences itself in good works."

Mission and Service. Again, the *Discipline*: "We insist that personal salvation always involves Christian mission and service to the world."

And finally, *Nurture and Mission of the Church.* "We emphasize the nurturing and serving function of Christian fellowship in the Church. The personal experience of faith is nourished by the worshiping community."

Are you getting a point here? We United Methodists do not say that one can believe anything one chooses, just so one believes in something. No, we hold to many of the things other Christians hold dear, but we also emphasize some dimensions of faith in special ways.

But we United Methodists are not content merely to cling to these basic beliefs, important as they are. Each of us is called to the "theological task" of expressing and articulating ever more clearly our relationship with God because by so doing we are better equipped to communicate with others and, as the *Discipline* states, "more fully prepared to participate in God's work in the world" (this quotation and those in the following paragraphs are from ¶ 104 of the *Discipline*).

We as United Methodists undertake that theological task, that task of clarifying and describing our understanding of our relationship with God, according to several premises, again described in the *Discipline*.

For example, "our theological task is both critical and constructive." That the task is "critical" means we are constantly evaluating our theology for clarity, truthfulness, and a genuine expression of love and grace; that it is "constructive" means we must make our theology ever new for an ever-changing world and world situation.

"Our theological task is both individual and communal." As individuals we test our understandings of God and responses to God within the community, and the community tests its understandings and responses with its individuals.

"Our theological task is contextual and incarnational." We believe that God revealed God's self in Christ Jesus, and so our theology is relevant to a particular time and situation. We live in a real world, and we are called to see Christ within and as part of the reality of the world in which we live.

And our theological work must be "essentially practical. It informs the individual's daily decisions and serves the Church's life and work."

So what tools do we have at our disposal as we go about this theological task, as we reflect theologically on the questions and concerns of each day and age?

The *Book of Discipline* tells us that we have four tools, and these tools, too, are part of the uniqueness of United Methodism.

The first tool we have to use when we do theology is the Holy Bible. "Scripture is the primary source and criterion for Christian doctrine." Remember what Wesley said about Scripture—that it contains all things necessary for salvation? We cannot think theologically without Scripture.

But Scripture is illuminated by a second tool, tradition. We are talking here of the traditions of Christianity, those understandings, practices, insights, and beliefs that have stood the test of time, of centuries of belief and understanding. We do not build theology in a vacuum; two thousand years of tradition add to our understanding.

A third tool is experience. We believe that God is a self-revealing God and that each of us has experiences of God over and over again. We test the validity of what we believe are experiences of God by what we learn from the community of faith and from Scripture and tradition. But it is our personal experiences of God through the Holy Spirit that help us recognize God's will for our lives.

And human reason is a fourth tool we use in doing theology. While human reason is not superior to all else, God has given each of us the ability to think for ourselves, to ponder the Scriptures, to reflect on traditions and on our own experiences, and to maintain open minds to new truths of the Gospel.

No, we have not answered those two questions at the start of the chapter completely; perhaps they can never be answered fully this side of the presence of God. But we United Methodists are called to think and reflect theologically, to determine action and response based on our understandings of God's will for our lives and the life of the world, and to grow in Christian faith and discipleship through constant study of the Scriptures, tradition, and our own experience.

Welcome, Lay Speaker, to a lifelong quest for a deeper and richer understanding of God's relationship with all that God has created, including (and especially!) you!

Called to Proclaim the Gospel Through Worship Leadership

3

You are called to proclaim the gospel. The first thing many think of in terms of proclamation is preaching. But before preaching, you will often be invited to participate, to assist, and to lead in other parts of a service of worship. And you are called to the proclamation of the gospel in this way just as surely as you are called to proclaim the gospel of Jesus Christ through preaching.

Two vital references

Be sure you have a copy of *The United Methodist Hymnal*. If you do not own your own copy, ask to borrow one from your church. We will be making many references to the *Hymnal* in this session.

Also, arrange to borrow a copy of *The United Methodist Book of Worship*; you may find this in your church library, or you can borrow it from your pastor. Ready?

Worship involves everyone

A service of worship, whether it is a typical Sunday morning service or any other kind, is a corporate activity in which all attendants participate. Sounds obvious, but it is not. In other words, Sunday morning worship is not a spectator sport; worship is active participation. Participation is more than passively sitting and listening; few of us truly worship when someone is talking to us. True worship occurs when the individual places the personal praises, confessions, supplications, intercessions, and grateful acknowledgment of the lordship of Jesus Christ before God. As you are called on to plan or to lead in worship, remember that your task is to invite and enable each worshiper to participate in the worship and praise of God, not to watch leaders go through some motions for them.

Worship: An integrated, cohesive whole

What goes into a worship service? How do you go about planning to lead a congregation in praising God? First, the formula of a couple of hymns, a prayer, and a sermon is no longer adequate—if it ever was. Worship must be planned with care and prayer so that all, including the worship leader, may experience God's presence and deepen their relationships with God through Jesus Christ. Second, although worship advisers of the past used to counsel planning a variety of elements in the service of worship, hoping that one or two might strike a responsive chord in each worshiper, that style is now

considered inadequate. A worship service must be an integrated, cohesive whole that leads up to a natural high. And that high is not the sermon; it is each worshiper's response to the experience of the presence of God through praise and worship. It is a big order.

Our denomination has provided excellent resources for planning and participating in worship. *The United Methodist Hymnal* is one of these. Besides knowing the "Index of First Lines and Common Titles of Hymns, Canticles and Acts of Worship" (pages 954–62), become familiar with the "Index of Topics and Categories" (pages 934–54) as you select hymns. The *Hymnal* contains more than excellent hymns; it is a rich and comprehensive worship resource.

On page 2 of the *Hymnal*, you will find "The Basic Pattern of Worship." Read the statements under each of the four elements: Entrance, Proclamation and Response, Thanksgiving and Communion, and Sending Forth. This is the basic outline of worship, the bare bones of an integrated and cohesive service of worship. On pages 3–5 of the *Hymnal*, you will find an order of worship that explains the four elements in more detail. Let's take a look at each element.

The Entrance

The Entrance has at least three parts: the Gathering, the Greeting and Hymn, and the Opening Prayers and Praise. The Gathering is when the people of God, the community of faith, come together in the presence of one another and of God to worship and praise God. It is somewhat informal. This is the time for announcements, for greeting one another, for news of the congregation. (Putting announcements in the midst of the service destroys the flow of the worship.)

The transition from the Gathering to the Greeting and Hymn is important. Invite worshipers to join in a quiet time of meditation and preparation during the prelude. The Greeting announces God's presence and welcomes worshipers. (See *The United Methodist Book of Worship*, pages 17–18, for more information.) Praise God through a hymn of adoration, proclaiming God's presence within the congregation and proclaiming God's sovereignty. Possible selections include hymns listed under "The Glory of the Triune God" (*Hymnal*, pages 57–152) and those listed under the heading "In Praise of Christ" (*Hymnal*, pages 153–94).

The Opening Prayers and Praise phase should include

an invocation, a prayer that invites God to be present. Invocations may be prayed by the congregation (involve the participants early), by a worship leader, or by a person from the congregation. (Also see the *Book of Worship*, pages 20–21, for suggested prayers.) Many congregations follow the invocation with a congregational affirmation of faith (*Hymnal*, 880–89) and the *Gloria Patri* (*Hymnal*, 70–71). Together these further unite the congregation in a sense of commonness of purpose (the affirmation) and praise (the *Gloria Patri*).

The Proclamation and Response

In how many ways can the Word of God be proclaimed? Reading Scripture and preaching a sermon are obvious, but are there other ways?

There are many creative and engaging options that can involve people from within the congregation. A member can lead the congregation in a responsive reading (*Hymnal*, pages 738–862) or paraphrase a scriptural passage. Music proclaims the Word of God. (Position anthems, solos, and other special music carefully and thoughtfully, paying special attention to the theme expressed in the piece and relating it to the service element.) Drama, liturgical dance, and multimedia presentations are other innovative ways to proclaim the Word of God. Whatever the form, there must always be an opportunity to open the Scripture within the Proclamation.

The Response of the people is not just to the sermon, but also to the entire experience of being in God's presence, of praising God, and of hearing the Word of God proclaimed. The response may also be in many forms, but it should always include some way of inviting people to a deeper commitment to Christian discipleship. This may include a formal invitation to discipleship. It may also be a call for silent prayer and commitment, a hymn of commitment (with an opportunity for personal involvement, such as through silent prayer at the communion rail), or any of the rituals listed on page 4 of the *Hymnal*. Note that a creed or affirmation of faith may be substituted if not used earlier in the service.

As part of the Response to the presence and Word of God, the congregation unites in prayer for self and for one another. This is the time when the congregation, as the community of Christ, responds to the presence of God by lifting joys and concerns. This is a time for the congregation to thank God for individual blessings and to seek God's presence in individual concerns. This may happen through a pastoral prayer, a prayer from a member of the congregation, a bidding prayer (people are invited to pray for whatever they wish, with the congregation saying afterward, "Lord, hear our prayer" or some other such phrase), or an appropriate choir anthem, special music, or a hymn.

Always include confession and pardon as part of the Response. This is an acknowledgment that we are sinners in need of God's grace-filled forgiveness and the procla-mation that we are recipients of that forgiveness. This can be included as part of the pastoral prayer, a congregational prayer spoken in unison, a prayer led by a member of the congregation, a hymn, an anthem, or special music. See the *Hymnal* (890–93) for what should be included in this crucial section of the service and for printed prayers of confession, assurance, and pardon. Confession and pardon must be focused, clear, personal, and real. As liturgist, you have the joy of announcing forgiveness to the congregation through God's name, fulfilling God's promise that they are forgiven!

The Offering is a continuing part of the response to God's presence and the Word of God. It is a tangible response to the presence of God and to the Word of God in the midst of the people. In many ways, the service of worship has focused on what God has done and is doing for us. The Offering is our small way of responding to God's blessings through God's presence, the Word of God, and the forgiveness of God. People can offer much more than financial support during the Offering. Make the Offering a time when people can offer their talents, their time, their prayers, and their selves as well as their resources. The offertory prayer and doxology (*Hymnal*, 94–95) acknowledge God as the source of all that we have and all that we are. They give us an opportunity to praise God again for all God is and does.

Thanksgiving and Communion

Through varied media such as a prayer, an anthem, a hymn, or special music, we again confess God's majesty, glory, and infinite love for each of us. This attitude is effectively summarized in the service of Holy Communion. But if Holy Communion is not to be observed on a particular Sunday, choose one of the many other forms of praising God.

The Sending Forth

The Sending Forth is a hymn of challenge and commitment to live as God directs in the coming days, and a benediction (or blessing) on the congregation. (See hymns listed in "Closing Hymns," page 939 of the *Hymnal*.) Consider encouraging your congregation to learn and sing several of the benediction choruses (*Hymnal*, 663–73).

Planning for worship is an awesome task that demands prayer and careful organization by the liturgist and preacher, as well as a detailed consideration of the Scriptures, the prayers, and the hymns and anthems that will focus the worship into an integrated and cohesive whole.

Scrutinize your worship outline, keeping in mind practical considerations such as the congregation's rhythm of activity. Extended periods of sitting and listening need to be broken by opportunities to stand and sing or to participate in a responsive reading or some other form of direct involvement. Unless you must conduct the service by yourself, it is best for the congregation to hear a variety of sounds: your voice, their voices, their voices singing, the voices of the choir, the instrumental music, and (very importantly) the sound of silence through which God speaks.

Do not neglect creature comforts. Is the worship space comfortably heated or cooled? Can everyone hear your voice and the voices of the other participants? Can everyone see the focal point of the worship service: the Communion Table and the cross? Does everyone have access to copies of *The United Methodist Hymnal*, printed prayers, or other congregational materials needed for the service?

Leading or participating in a service of worship is a high and holy task, which demands the best you have to offer. Never, never dismiss the role of liturgist by thinking that the preacher is the more significant person and that the sermon is the most important element of the worship. And never lead in a service of worship without first consulting with those who will be choosing the text for the sermon. Work closely in advance with those people to ensure an integrated and cohesive service. This is why, except on special occasions, asking the congregation to suggest favorite hymns or just reading some favorite Scriptures interferes with the flow of worship.

God has called you to proclaim the Word of God through participating in leading a congregation in worship. No higher calling is possible!

Called to Proclaim the Gospel Through Preaching

4

"I'm going to be out of town three weeks from Sunday—that's the eighteenth. Can you preach for me?"

"How about preaching on the twenty-sixth? That's the DISCIPLE Bible study retreat, and I'll be at our conference camp with our three DISCIPLE groups."

"Would you be able to present the chapel service message at the nursing home next week?"

Called to proclaim the gospel? Can you do it?

Proclaiming the gospel has a variety of meanings and takes many forms. Historically, lay speaking began as a lay preaching movement. Over the years, the role and function of the lay speaker has expanded and broadened. But one of the basic functions, perhaps the one that attracted you to this opportunity in the first place, was preaching.

Preaching takes place in many different places and under many different circumstances. A few scenarios are illustrated at the beginning of this chapter. Often, a lay speaker's preaching takes place at the Sunday morning worship service in the lay speaker's own church—sometimes with much advance notice, sometimes with last-minute notice. Preaching also takes place when a lay speaker is called to lead worship for an organization within the church (United Methodist Men or United Methodist Women meetings), for a community-wide ecumenical service (celebrating Thanksgiving or World Day of Prayer), or for Sunday school classes or worship services in public facilities (nursing homes, hospitals, or prisons). In our community, a major weekend-long community festival has a lay-led ecumenical outdoor worship service at a festival grounds.

Undoubtedly, lay speakers are called to proclaim the gospel of Jesus Christ through preaching!

Whether you have preached a number of times or have never preached at all, this chapter will lead you through the basics of planning, preparing, and delivering a sermon. If you are experienced, this will count as a review. If you have never preached, this may be a good place to start on what could be an extraordinary journey.

The invitation for you to preach arrives. Do you feel panicked? Good! Preaching the Word of God is an awesome responsibility that demands the very best of us. It should make us feel anxious, since we will be addressing the eternal souls of people. Some of the nation's best preachers have anxiety attacks before a service. One has declared that he will stop preaching when he no longer feels anxious, because he fears that, if that time comes,

he might not be taking the responsibility as seriously as he should.

You accept the invitation to preach. Start your preparation with prayer. (Continue that prayer until you are on your way home from the preaching assignment. At that time, change the prayer to one of thanksgiving for God's presence with you during the experience.)

So, what will you preach about?

Traditionally, preaching has fallen into two general categories: biblical and topical. In biblical preaching, you choose a scriptural text and discuss it and its teachings as your sermon. In topical preaching, you select a topic, issue, or concern, then build your sermon around it, illustrating and expanding your points through the use of the Bible.

Yes, the Bible is basic in both approaches!

Biblical preaching through the Lectionary

A lectionary is a Sunday-by-Sunday list of biblical passages. The *Revised Common Lectionary* contains four readings for each Sunday: one from the Old Testament, a psalm (or portion of a psalm), a lesson from an Epistle, and a Gospel lesson. It was developed by representatives from many denominations and is made available in a variety of forms. Using the Lectionary ensures that the preacher does not preach only about his or her favorite texts but includes all of the Bible.

If the church where you will preach uses the Lectionary regularly, or if you decide to use it yourself, you need to identify the readings for the Sunday you will be preaching. *The United Methodist Book of Worship* (pages 227–37) lists the Lectionary readings for every Sunday through the year 2020. You will be able to determine the set of readings you should use (A, B, or C) by referring to the beginning of the lists. For example:

- Year B: Advent 2005
- Year C: Advent 2006
- Year A: Advent 2007
- Year B: Advent 2008

Some people who use the Lectionary use all four readings for each Sunday sermon. That is a difficult task! Many preachers use one or two of the readings as the basis for their sermons. It is perfectly appropriate to build an entire sermon around one Lectionary reading. (Some base their sermons on only the Gospel lesson, because it is often easier to develop a sermon from a Gospel passage.)

Preparing the message

Whether you choose to use the Lectionary readings or Scriptures appropriate to your topic, read each of the biblical texts prayerfully. Study the context of each reading. What happens before and after this passage? What is the setting in which this passage takes place? Study the footnotes listed in your Bible that refer to these passages; check commentaries for additional ideas and insights. Your pastor or Christian educator can help you locate helpful resources.

After choosing a passage (or passages), determine the point you wish to make. Notice we said point, not points. Do not be bound by the three-points-and-a-poem model. How much better to make a single solid point than three weak points. How much better to get your listeners inside the Scripture rather than using it as a springboard for your own ideas.

Chose a point carefully. That point should be within the Scripture, and it must relate to the everyday lives of the listeners. The point should be direct, clear, and concise. Some preachers say it must be a point that can be made in several different ways within the sermon so the listener cannot help getting it.

Finally, make your point a point of good news. That is what the gospel is; it is the good news of God's forgiveness, love, and grace. Pointing out our failures, our sinfulness, our unfaithfulness may be necessary, but the climax must focus on the ultimate good news of the gospel of Jesus Christ. Inherent in the good news is the challenge to live more completely for Jesus Christ than ever before. Part of the good news is the challenge to be renewed and recommitted to what life brings.

Test your point before making a final decision. Talk with a trusted and honest friend. Describe the Scripture you plan to use and the point you plan to make. Let the friend critique your idea. Does it work? Does it make sense? Does the point flow naturally from the Scripture, or are you forcing the Scripture to say something it really does not say? Honest feedback at this point will save hours of work later.

Now develop your sermon. Think in three areas or dimensions: presenting the Scripture, introducing your point, and connecting the point and the Scripture so that it touches the lives of the listeners. Explain the background of the Scripture so that your listeners can fully understand your point. For example, the neighborliness of the good Samaritan (Luke 10:25-37) is more understandable if you explain how the first-century Jews and Samaritans reviled one another. The parable of the talents (Matthew 25:14-30) takes on new meaning if your listeners understand that a single talent represented fifteen years of wages for a worker.

In communicating your message, how will you introduce your point, make it, and reinforce it? For instance, what reminders about everyday life do your listeners need to tune into your point? An example: Do people need to be reminded that we all make false gods out of many things: possessions, riches, and so on? Do people need the reminder that all of us break our covenant with God by our own prideful actions?

Once you are satisfied with the point and the way you want to communicate it, you are ready to construct the sermon. As you design the message, remember that you must engage the listeners. Get their attention. To do this, you may want to tell a story related to your point or retell the Scripture. Connect with your audience so that they will follow you to your point. When you make the point, offer your listeners the good news of Jesus Christ and invite them to respond. Response may include a first-time profession of faith, a reaffirmation of faith, or an action based on the message they received. God's Word always asks us, "Now what?" Be sure that your message invites a response.

Now it's time

It is your decision: an outline or a manuscript. Many people start with an outline, then do a full manuscript. You will make changes in your outline as a result of your manuscript; then you will revise your manuscript as you change your outline. Do not be afraid of brief stories; people relate well to stories. But avoid jokes and humorous anecdotes. Few preachers can tell jokes in the pulpit well, and jokes often detract from the point you are trying to make.

Now practice your presentation. Will you preach from notes or from a manuscript? We suggest using a manuscript for the first sermons; do not read it, of course, but have it with you in the pulpit, with main emphases underlined or highlighted. Go over the sermon, practice it until you have it down perfectly, then go over it some more.

Practice in front of your family or a friend and in front of a mirror. A humbling but eye-opening self-appraisal can come from videotaping and viewing one of your practice sessions. Check your voice, your gestures, your emphases. Also check your grammar. Good messages can be ruined by bad grammar, mispronunciation of biblical names and places, or poor command of the language.

The day has come and you think you are ready. As you approach the time for the message, you may be struck by two fears: you really have not mastered what you want to say, and what you had planned to say is completely wrong for this congregation. If this happens, trust that you have been guided by God throughout your preparation and that God will touch hearts through the Holy Spirit's power. Your prayer may be, "God, not through me or because of me but in spite of me, let these people hear your Word."

As you begin, your voice may sound strange to you. After a few sentences, release your grip on the pulpit and feel free to use the gestures you practiced. You are a friend telling your friends how to enrich their lives by knowing Jesus Christ as Lord. Rely on your manuscript; read portions that you want to be sure you say just right. Ignore the clock. Do not worry that your sermon is not long enough or that it is too long. Know that God is with you in your planning, in your preparation, and in your preaching. Trust God.

Here are some suggestions as a postscript: Do not ask for immediate feedback about your sermon after the service. People leaving the church will compliment you. Take this with a grain of salt. Trusted friends and your spouse will compliment you after the sermon; ignore this too. After twenty-four hours, go to your spouse or to some trusted friends and ask for comments on the content, structure, and interest level of the sermon. Ask them to comment on your delivery voice, gestures, speed of delivery, and all of the rest. Impress on these trusted ones that you are seeking their input to better serve God and that endless compliments are not instructive.

Keep this in mind: The hearer is as much a part of the sermon as the preacher!

Called to Proclaim the Gospel Through Witnessing

5

Witnessing is not easy. Many pastors have said they would rather preach a dozen sermons than make a cold call on an unchurched family. Pastors do not always know what to say either!

Speaking before a group of people is one thing; it is threatening and exciting, all at the same time. But sharing our personal and individual faith with someone—some people use the word *witnessing*—is quite another. Talking one-on-one about matters of the faith can summon a whole different set of anxieties.

Some think witnessing is telling another person how to live or what to believe. They think witnessing includes judging another's life. But we understand witnessing to mean sharing God in Jesus Christ and expressing how you, the speaker, have experienced God's love and grace. Witnessing may include inviting someone to know Christ as you do, but it does not have to. You ask, "Will this person think I am being self-righteous?" Not if your witness is filled with a humble Christian spirit.

But as a Christian, and especially as a lay speaker, you will be asked through opportunity and assignment to share your faith and to represent the church in one-on-one situations. You may be asking, "What will I say?" It has been the question of everyone who ever tried to share the Christian faith.

Yet, God calls on each of us to proclaim the gospel of Jesus Christ through witnessing and testifying. (Let us not be afraid of some of the traditional words of the Christian faith!)

OPPORTUNITIES TO WITNESS

A nursing home

You have been asked to call on several people at a local nursing home. What do you say? Most of us would ask the person how she or he is doing, make some comment about the facility or room in which the person lives, talk about the weather, or comment about family photos displayed in the room. Through these small gestures, you will bring a little cheer to the person, and both you and the individual will feel better for it.

But, have you represented your congregation? Have you proclaimed the gospel of Jesus Christ as you are called to do? Have you, in any sense, testified or witnessed to that person?

Keep in mind that you are visiting as a representative of Christ's church. This means that you visit with a clear message and a spiritual presence that other organizations do not bring. You are there in the name of Jesus Christ and in the name of your congregation. So what do you do?

First, you bear the Christian witness by your presence. Being there in the name of Christ and the church is an eloquent witness and testimony. "I'm here from Wesley United Methodist Church" sets the context.

Then, you listen. You listen carefully and intently, asking in silent prayer that God will allow you to discern how your witness may help this person at this moment. Ask simple questions that cannot be answered with a yes or no. You can begin with the small talk—the weather, the family photos, how the person is feeling—to establish a comfortable relationship. Nothing makes another person more comfortable than sensing that you are actively listening, giving your undivided (and nonjudgmental) attention.

Listen for statements or comments for which you can praise God and which suggest prayers of intercession, that is, prayers for other people. Listen for joys and sorrows, victories and frustrations that you can place before the Lord in a prayer together. Through listening, you can make your witness to that individual both personal and vital.

Recalling God's presence

Often, our witnessing is impeded by our inability to introduce the presence of God. Sometimes visitors make the small talk, move to the heavy stuff or God talk, pray, and are out of there. How much better if we engage in conversation with that woman or man, gently pointing out the activity and revelation of God in the everyday life of that person. Many long to be reminded that God has not forgotten them. Pointing out God's presence from what the nursing home resident is telling you communicates the presence of God in that very setting.

But is not witnessing sharing faith? Yes, but often the dimension of faith that you share is how you experience God's presence in your life each day. Sharing your faith means witnessing to how you have come to discover God's care and concern.

Caution: This is not an opportunity to pour out your personal issues on the nursing home resident. But it is an opportunity for you to identify with that person and to describe, briefly and joyfully, how you have encountered God in situations similar to those experienced by that person.

Always have a prayer together. Do not feel that you have to leave this until the end. Pray together several times during the visit. Ask the person to pray silently or to pray with you, even reciting the Lord's Prayer together. Avoid using only written prayers; use simple and personal prayers in which you mention the individual you are visiting and perhaps the person's family members by name. Hold his or her hand while you are praying because you will minister through the act of physical contact. (Be sensitive to any discomfort that squeezing a hand or pulling on an arm might cause.)

Should you read from the Bible when you make a pastoral visit to someone? Take a Bible with you and be prepared with selected verses. You may want to ask about the person's favorite verses. But do not feel that you must read, especially if reading does not fit in with the direction of your conversation.

A lot to remember? Perhaps. Trust that God will be with you and give you the words you need as you witness.

Hospital visits

Most of what we said about visiting people in nursing homes also goes for hospital visits. Keep these visits brief, especially if the patient is quite ill. Be extra careful in touching the patient; limbs can be tender or sore from treatments. And, perhaps most importantly, listen!

Many times a patient may want to talk about her or his illness and about the fears and anxieties that accompany being in the hospital. Sometimes our tendency is to say something cheerful such as, "You'll be up and out of here in a couple days." Often, that is not what the patient needs to hear. She or he may want to hear the silence of a friend in Christ who is listening honestly and intently and is willing to accept what the patient says without judgment, without denial, and, during severe illness, without false or empty promises of a return to complete health.

Again, do not hesitate to introduce the presence of God. Indicate your Christian witness through prayer early in the visit. Make your prayer a reflection of the conversation, and again offer several brief prayers during the visit.

To what dimensions of the gospel of Jesus Christ do you witness in a hospital room? Witness not to Christ the miracle-working healer, for we cannot promise that. But we can promise Emmanuel: God is with us, God is here now, God has not deserted those who are ill, and God is present with the person who is ill.

Are you getting the idea? The most effective witnessing is through presence and listening. Our response is one of gently reminding the person of God's presence and God's love.

When there is a death

A church member has died, and you go to visit the family. What do you say?

Often, the best thing to say is little or nothing. Again, your presence and attentive listening to the bereaved will speak most eloquently. We recall being at a funeral home when church members came to console a young mother whose husband had died without warning. Dozens of people offered condolences; many had thought carefully about what they were going to say and said it well. Then there was Mary, a town character, in the line waiting to see the young mother. Because she has a reputation for being loud, boisterous, and aggressively opinionated, some of us worried that the young mother did not need to see her. But when Mary's turn came, all she did was embrace the young woman gently and wordlessly as their tears mingled. Mary moved on almost immediately. Months later, the young mother told us that the sounds of Mary gently weeping with her were far more eloquent and comforting than all of the words the other visitors, including the preacher, had offered her that evening. In many situations, our presence speaks far more loudly than all our well-chosen words.

In later visits, family members often want to talk about the person they have lost. While we may be uncomfortable and wish to shift the subject, this conversation may be an important part of healing. Again, listen and assure the person of God's presence and love. That is our witness and our Christian testimony in such a time.

Witnessing to and with friends

This brings us to what may be the most difficult kind of witnessing: witnessing to our friends, our coworkers, those we see every day—including our family members!

We have all had experiences with well-meaning people who almost drove us away by their persistent quoting of the Bible and advice about how to live our lives. But that is not the kind of witnessing and testifying we are talking about here.

We want to urge lay speakers to engage in a witness of life and lifestyle that reflects the presence of Jesus Christ. Who we are and what we do is a far more eloquent witness than all of our words combined, for others are watching to see if we truly walk the walk as well as talk the talk. We witness through our presence, our love, our compassion, and our willingness to listen and to try to understand. We witness in response to the particular opening provided by the person to whom we are witnessing.

A story is told about a famous theologian who was once asked by a seminary student how to witness. The theologian, in order to make his point, told the young student to go to the most destitute part of town, to enter the seediest bar he could find, and to sit down with the loneliest-appearing, most helpless-looking individual he could find. The theologian said simply, "Sit there. Don't say anything. Just be there." Then the theologian said, "Go back the next night and the next night and the next night and simply sit in silence with that individual. One night that individual will say to you, 'Why? Why do you come here night after night to sit with me? Why do you leave your home and all your comforts to come here to be with me?'"

"Then," said the theologian, "you can tell that person about the Christ who came and sat with you night after night, surrounding you with his presence and his love, and planted within you a burning desire to share that love with others."

Presence. Listening. Readiness. Meeting the other person where he or she is. That is effective witnessing.

That is testifying to the love of God in Jesus Christ. In fact, that is exactly what God did for us.

A promise

There is no joy like the joy that comes from sharing the gospel of Jesus Christ one-on-one.

Try it. And know that God's presence will be with you.

Called to Proclaim the Gospel Through Teaching

6

As a lay speaker in The United Methodist Church, you are called to proclaim the gospel in many different ways. We have mentioned worship leadership, preaching, and witnessing. Perhaps most often you will proclaim the gospel through teaching.

The ministry of teaching is a sacred ministry; some would argue that Jesus spent much more time teaching than he did preaching. The earliest church listed teachers among its most responsible positions, and Jesus' final charge to his disciples, according to Matthew, was to go into all the world teaching.

Teaching is preaching is teaching

You might counter the above with, "Isn't good preaching teaching?" The answer is a resounding yes. In one sense, all preaching is teaching, but teaching is the larger of the two categories. In other words, teaching includes preaching, but it also includes a number of other activities and ministries as well. Preaching is a part of teaching; preaching is one way we teach. But teaching through preaching is not the only avenue open to the lay speaker.

Confused about these words and terms? There is some overlap. But let us draw some distinctions between teaching and preaching. (Yes, these distinctions are not absolute; and, yes, some may be exaggerated here to make the point.)

In preaching, the preacher speaks to a basically passive group of people. While the preacher can gauge how the sermon is being received by the body language and facial expressions, seldom does the congregation engage in dialogue with the preacher or provide any ongoing feedback. In teaching, on the other hand, the teacher is engaged with a group of people who are actively involved with the teacher. The learners respond to the teacher: They ask for clarification; they agree, disagree, argue; and they make their own points. Most often, teaching is an activity in which both teacher and learners are actively involved.

In preaching, the preacher determines what the content will be and deals with that content in the sermon. In teaching, the good teacher selects the content for the session, but the ongoing interaction with the students may redirect that content, refocus the session, or limit the number of points the teacher can cover. For example, a preacher may plan to make two points in a sermon and will make these points within the allotted time, without interruption or input from the listeners. The teacher, on the other hand, may plan to make three points during a session but quickly discover that the first point has engendered so much discussion, so much need for clarification and illustration, that the teacher focuses on the first point for the entire session.

A preacher comes to the pulpit as the informed authority. She or he has the attention of the congregation to tell them something and is likely to lead them to some informed conclusions or actions. That is, the preacher is unlikely to learn from the group to whom he or she is preaching because of the lack of interaction and feedback (other than expressions and body language). But the teacher learns constantly from the group through the interaction, the questions, the comments, and the requests for clarification. If you have ever taught Sunday school, you know you learn far more from the students than you teach them! In teaching, there is a sense of co-discovery that is not always present in preaching.

But the teacher and the preacher are also similar in many significant ways. Both have exactly the same purpose or goal in mind: to help people grow in their relationship with God through Jesus Christ and to help them identify and live out their discipleship in the world.

Both preachers and teachers must be committed to the tasks before them; both must have a passion for the gospel of Jesus Christ and an earnest desire to help people grow more Christlike every day. Note: This does not mean that either or both must be biblical scholars or master theologians. But both must be willing to study to equip themselves for their tasks, and both must be willing to grow in their own relationship with God through Jesus Christ. Remember, John Wesley was once told to "preach faith *till* you have it; and then, *because* you have it, you *will* preach faith" (from an entry under March 4, 1738, in the journal of John Wesley). Neither the preacher nor the teacher is the perfect Christian, but both must be constantly striving toward greater commitment to Jesus Christ as Lord and constantly learning along the way.

Both teachers and preachers must be willing to share their own faith stories and their own struggles within the Christian faith. Remember that part of our faith stories are the times when our faith has been weak or when we have been unfaithful. Neither the preacher nor the teacher is an individual who has arrived; both are pilgrims on the journey of faith, just like those they seek to lead.

Both preachers and teachers must know the people to whom they are preaching or teaching. Neither operates in a vacuum; both depend upon a careful knowledge and understanding of the people involved. Fantastic sermons or great Sunday school lessons from one church may fall flat at another church. The difference is the people! (Hint: This is why we suggest you avoid recycling sermons or lessons, unless you carefully adapt them for the differences in the congregation and the setting.)

Both teachers and preachers try to reach the whole person. By that we mean that each of us learns and grows through different ways of learning: cognitive (facts), affective (feelings and attitudes), psychomotor (physical movement), social (relationships), and imaginative. A good preacher may be able to appeal to all of these learning receptors, but a good teacher can use each of these fully in the varied settings and interaction of the classroom.

Sunday school, study groups, and midweek classes

So, where and when does the lay speaker teach? The answer is anytime, anywhere! The most obvious place is within your congregation's Sunday school. If you are not currently teaching a Sunday school class, consider volunteering to teach one. What better way is there to share your faith and help others grow in their faith and discipleship? And do not limit yourself to adults. Try teaching preschoolers, children, youth, young adults, singles, older adults. By teaching diversified groups, you will become more effective in helping all people grow in faith and discipleship. And teaching a group of people who are quite unlike you in age, lifestyle, or perspective will be a rich experience for all of you.

You may say, "I'm superintendent of the Sunday school or chair of the work area on education." Fine. But administering a teaching program is not the same as actually teaching. We urge you to make arrangements to teach on a regular basis. You may already know that the discipline of preparing a lesson each week is one of the best ways to keep your own faith vital and growing.

Do not, however, limit your teaching to Sunday morning. Seek opportunities to teach through the week as well. Intensive Bible studies such as DISCIPLE provide you with rich opportunities to teach and to learn in the midst of deeply committed Christians. The DISCIPLE training experience is spiritually energizing. Consider organizing special short-term study groups around specific topics, or initiate seasonal studies (in cooperation with the nurture committee or work area on education). Seek out the teaching opportunities presented by United Methodist Women, United Methodist Men, United Methodist Youth Fellowship, and committee meetings where you can use a portion of the gathering as a teaching-learning time to enrich your membership, practice your teaching techniques, and expand the knowledge of your entire congregation.

Help for the beginning teacher

Not sure you know how to teach? Check out the list of resources at the end of this manual for some good books on teaching. But books alone do not substitute for the experience and skills developed by participating in annual conference laboratory schools or teacher training events.

Recall good teachers you have known. What characteristics can you list? Identify good teachers in your midst; observe them as you learn from them.

Keep in mind that good teachers are

- constantly learning;
- well-prepared and punctual;
- always concerned for the person as well as the content;
- personally invested in the topic;
- using varied teaching-learning styles;
- seeking feedback and growth opportunities.

Avail yourself of every opportunity to become a better teacher, for you will be more effective in your proclamation of the gospel of Jesus Christ.

One-on-one teaching

One-on-one teaching is teaching one other person or learning from one other person: a class of two. Many churches use this approach, especially to assimilate new members or to prepare youth for confirmation. One-on-one teachers are called many things—mentors, fellowship friends, friends in faith, spiritual guides, co-travelers, or co-seekers, to cite a few. All mean essentially the same thing: You become responsible for guiding and directing another's growth in faith and discipleship, and, by so doing, you discover how greatly your own life of faith and discipleship is enriched and renewed.

One-on-one teaching gives you an opportunity to know another person well. Through formal sessions and informal times together, you both probe and share and grow in the richest kind of Christian education possible. People who have served as mentors report that both the mentor and the student grow immeasurably in Christian faith and discipleship through the closeness of the spiritual relationship. Do not pass up an opportunity to be the fellowship friend or mentor to a youth or newcomer; you would miss a rich spiritual experience.

Resources for teaching and learning

Since most of us are not biblical scholars or theologians, studying the Bible without the guidance of a study book is difficult and often incomplete. Curriculum resources, both for the student and the teacher, give invaluable guidance in both understanding the message of the Scripture and in applying it to our lives. Those resources are listed in our United Methodist Discipleship Resources or Cokesbury catalogs (either in print or online) or can be found at Cokesbury bookstores. In addition, there are many excellent resources in local Christian bookstores.

Relationship first, lesson second

Still not convinced? If you grew up in Sunday school, what is your earliest memory? a song you learned? a storybook? a take-home paper? If you are like most others, your earliest memory is of a person, a teacher, who loved you in a special way and helped you experience the love and presence of Jesus Christ. That teacher demonstrated Christ's love to you, and taught through love and living. Most people remember the person more than the lessons; but through that person, they grew to know and love Jesus Christ. That is why teaching is so important. And that is why your call to proclaim the gospel of Jesus Christ as a lay speaker is a call to teaching.

Called to Proclaim the Gospel Through Leadership

The ability to lead is a gift from God to be used to God's glory and to bring others to a living relationship with God through Jesus Christ. It is a gift that reflects God and God's will for God's people.

You may be a leader already in your congregation, in your district and annual conference, in your community, or in your work. You have probably already demonstrated leadership skills and abilities. Therefore, we are not going to discuss how to be a leader in terms of visioning, motivating, organizing, negotiating, delegating, monitoring, and all of those other leadership skills that are so crucial.

Instead, we will list leadership characteristics emerging from the Scriptures and relate these to leadership in the present. We will list these by using an acrostic—the first letter of each of these words spells the word *leader*.

Christian leaders demonstrate **loyalty**. Leaders are tenaciously loyal to the people they are called to lead. In some cases, being loyal to a cause or goal is almost easier than being loyal to a group of people.

God called Moses to lead the children of Israel, but they did not want to be led. They disobeyed, questioned, bickered, doubted, threatened, relapsed into old ways. Indeed, they tried everything to destroy Moses' sense of leadership. Moses became so frustrated at times that he called them stiff-necked, but he never gave up. He was loyal to the people despite their disloyalty. He passionately demonstrated God's love for the people and his own love for the sometimes-reluctant, ragtag, wandering band. In the end, Moses' tenacious loyalty paid off, both for Moses and for the people. Read all about it in the books of Exodus and Numbers.

We may often be tempted to lose patience with the people or congregation we are called to lead. Sometimes we are tempted to move on to greener pastures, to find a group that will follow us and to "give up on this group because they're never going to go anywhere." Usually, this happens when our feelings are hurt, when we have been misunderstood, or when people openly reject our leadership. Moses must have felt like that time and time again, but his loyalty to the people overcame his personal agenda and enabled him to follow God by leading his people as God directed.

A second characteristic of this kind of leadership is **energy**. This does not always mean the high-activity, rah-rah kind of energy, although a good leader knows there may be a time for that. We mean a fortitude to focus on the task at hand, employing all of the leader's innovative gifts and graces. Queen Esther of the Old Testament is a wonderful example of this kind of energy. Esther was not always what we often call a high-energy person. However, she displayed the kind of energy we are describing when she placed herself in a position to save her people from the evil that Haman was about to bring upon them. When one plan was not available to her, she created a second and a third, devoting herself entirely to the task at hand. How much easier life might have been for Esther had she quietly accepted her place as the new queen, remained obedient to the king, and forgotten the people from which she came. But she could not; her energy was devoted to saving her people.

The next crucial characteristic is **availability**. You have been in situations where God has called you for a task you did not really want to do (including, perhaps, being in this course right now), but you made yourself available to God. And because you did, God has used you (and will use you) in remarkable and significant ways.

Think about the fascinating biblical stories of availability. Remember that each of these people could have said no to God, but each heard God's call and made herself or himself available. Just a few examples:

Amos stated that he was not qualified when called by God: "I am no prophet, nor a prophet's son; but I am a herdsman, and a dresser of sycamore trees" (Amos 7:14). But God called, and Amos made himself available. "The lion has roared; who will not fear? The Lord GOD has spoken; who can but prophesy?" (Amos 3:8).

David was a youth in the fields, unaware that Samuel was seeking the Lord's anointed in Jesse's home. But David made himself available (1 Samuel 16).

And, what about the ordinary people who made themselves available to God? Remember the woman of Samaria who met Jesus at the well, then made herself available to proclaim the presence of God in the midst of the people (John 4:7-42)?

Zacchaeus, the curious doubter, made himself available by offering restitution to everyone whom he had wronged (Luke 19:1-10).

You have made yourself available to God and have been used by God, despite probable personal doubts, temporary ambitions, false starts, and other hindrances.

We have hinted at another characteristic. Many terms for this characteristic could be used, but we are using the word **dedication**. When we are dedicated to the call and vision of God, we can lead people in the right direction, not just any direction. Remember how the Hebrews wanted to go back to Egypt, but Moses was dedicated to the vision of the land flowing with milk and honey (Exodus 16:2-8)? Remember how Peter wanted to stay on the mountaintop with Jesus, but Jesus steadfastly led him and the other disciples to Jerusalem (Matthew 16:21–17:9)? Loyalty must be coupled with dedication to a greater vision, and that vision must have its genesis in God and God's call on our lives.

Elijah, Jeremiah, and Paul are good examples of this kind of dedication. Through incredible hardships, total rejection, great danger, and uncooperative and belligerent people, these spokespersons for God led their people by sheer determination and absolute dedication to the vision God had placed within them. How much easier it might have been for them to say, "These people will never understand; forget it!" or "I'll take this message to someone who will listen!" But these three, and countless others like them in the Scriptures and in the annals of Christian history, steadfastly clung to the vision God had given them for that time and for those people. Each remained totally dedicated to the call of God in his or her life and turned people around. Think what John Wesley did in England, despite the official and unofficial rejection he repeatedly received. His was a God-given vision for reaching the masses with the message of a personal gospel!

Our first *E* in this acrostic was *energy*; the second *E* is **enthusiasm**! Some significant differences between energy and enthusiasm are apparent: Energy is what the leader possesses to do her or his task; enthusiasm is what the leader conveys to the people to engage them in the vision. Most biblical leaders display this kind of challenging, motivating, inspiring enthusiasm, portraying the wide variety of ways enthusiasm can move a people.

Think of Deborah, in the Book of Judges, singing the praises of God after the defeat of Sisera and inspiring the people to go on with the conquest of the land that God had promised them (Judges 4:4–5:31). Think of Silas and Paul, chained in prison, singing hymns of thanksgiving to God and, by so doing, leading others in the dungeon to renew their faith in God (Acts 16:16-34).

But enthusiasm is not always outward, vocal, and obvious. The enthusiasm of Jesus as he set out toward Jerusalem was picked up by the apostles, who willingly followed him. The almost angry enthusiasm of Moses goaded the people into action when they most doubted. Enthusiasm is more than being a cheerleader. It is the ability to inspire and motivate others, and to invite them to respond to God's call. One hopes that this response will ultimately become the basis of their lives.

The *R* stands for the cost of being a leader, the price we pay in responding to God's call to lead: **risk**.

The biblical leaders took great risks to their reputations as well as to their lives. Paul's litany of all that had happened to him; Jeremiah thrown into the well; Elijah under a sentence of death; the heroes in the Book of Daniel—all of these and many others demonstrate the leader's willingness to risk personal danger for the sake of following God's call and direction.

No one suffered greater risk than the Lord Jesus Christ. The worst possible scenario of that risk was lived out in the arrest, trial, and crucifixion of Jesus Christ.

Called to lead by following

You are also called to ministries where you allow another to lead. Sometimes you need to encourage and support rather than be out front.

Learn to become a leader who does not need personal glory. Find achievement in reaching a group goal or objective. But what are the characteristics of this kind of following that are found in biblical examples?

Recall the history of the early church after the resurrection of Jesus Christ. The Acts of the Apostles are filled with stories of strong leaders and the dedicated and committed followers who made the task of the leadership doable. Peter was the obvious leader, but could he have carried out his ministry without the sure support of James and John? Paul was dynamic and charismatic, a leader in every sense of the word. But think how his ministry would have fallen short had he not been undergirded by the support of people such as Barnabas, Titus, Lydia, and Priscilla.

Look to the Old Testament for other examples. David, the outstanding leader, was supported by a host of people, including Jonathan, Nathan, Abigail, and many others. Moses had the support of Joshua and Caleb, who eventually became leaders. Each of these examples demonstrates the supporting-role qualities of discipleship.

The disciple who leads by following puts aside a personal agenda for the sake of proclaiming the gospel of the Savior. Obvious, right? But it is difficult! Often, we become so excited by and committed to our plan, idea, or concept that we become blind and deaf to alternatives. Perhaps we fail to see that our plan is not the whole story, but the gospel is!

One of the best principles of working as a congregation is summarized by the statement "We can do anything as long as we don't care who gets credit for it." That is the disciple's motto, because a supportive disciple knows when it is time to push for a personal idea and when it is time to surrender to the will of the group.

Peter fought against his own single-mindedness on a number of occasions. He wanted to build booths for those he saw on the Mount of Transfiguration. He argued with Jesus about going to Jerusalem, strongly counseling against it. He begged Jesus to wash his whole body, not just his feet, failing to understand the greater meaning of what the Savior was doing. But something inside of Peter helped him eventually to see that the cause, the gospel, was more than his own ideas, plans, and perceptions.

He ultimately surrendered to the will of God through Jesus Christ. And, despite all of the other qualities of character we know about the apostle Peter, we have no evidence that he pouted, sulked, or refused to support the direction that Jesus Christ was taking.

God forbid that a lay speaker in The United Methodist Church would do less. May God strengthen each of us to throw our wholehearted support and enthusiasm behind a plan, idea, or project not of our own making if it is the will of the congregation and truly moves in the direction of proclaiming the gospel of Jesus Christ.

Discipleship is also characterized by a kind of activism that moves things ahead, that stimulates and motivates others to act, and that challenges others to fulfill their responsibilities in a project that will further the gospel of Jesus Christ.

Have you ever heard the term "stuck on dead center?" In some congregational ministries, it may mean that all of the plans are in place, all of the organization completed, and all of the pieces in line—but, still, nothing happens.

Nothing happens because the group may be waiting for someone other than the leader to take the first step. Sometimes people are most impressed when one of their own can stimulate and challenge them to act.

The children of Israel faced this situation in the desert as they sought the Promised Land. In Deuteronomy 1:6-7, the Lord says to Moses and the people: "You have stayed long enough at this mountain. Resume your journey."

Sometimes we wander around our own mountains, going over the same plans and details again and again, but we never really start on the task at hand. Often, we are better at "we ought to" than we are at "let's do it!"

Jesus recognized this tendency. He warned that once we put our hand to the plow and turn back, we are not worthy of the kingdom of God. He consistently challenged the apostles to be doers of the word and not hearers only. Jesus, a man of action, called his apostles to be people of action; and, by extension, he calls us to be disciples of action.

Do not fear taking that first step, leading, and saying yes. Put wings and feet to plans laid by others. Picture the apostles of Jesus Christ days after the Resurrection and before the Day of Pentecost. Fearlessly and confidently they proclaimed Jesus as the Messiah, and they performed miracles in Jesus' name (Mark 16:20). How much easier for the disciples if they had waited to see if Jesus would return immediately. But they eagerly traveled throughout the known world with the message of forgiveness, redemption, hope, and promise. In short, disciples act—and act decisively—in the name of Jesus Christ.

As a lay speaker, you may not always be called to lead. You may be asked to play a supporting role. Never forget that performing a supporting role is one of the truest ways of bringing about the day when "every knee should bend . . . and every tongue should confess that Jesus Christ is Lord" (Philippians 2:10-11).

Called to Proclaim the Gospel Through Service

8

Whether you are the designated leader or are called upon to follow rather than lead, the nature of your response must be the same: to serve. Whatever else a Christian is called to be and to do, a Christian is primarily called to live as a servant. This is what the Lord Jesus Christ did.

Serving takes many forms. It means placing the will of God—and the good of others—ahead of self and personal desires. It means using who we are and what we are for the benefit of our sisters and brothers. To serve is to emulate Christ in words and in deeds.

One year when a hurricane struck southern Florida, teams of servant Christians rushed to Florida to assist. At one church a lay speaker announced that he was seeking others to go to Florida to help people recover and restore their lives. He asked for volunteers and asked them what they could provide for this special outreach effort. A plumber volunteered to go and help repair damaged water systems. Another said he could not go, but his hardware store would provide free nails, paint, and other supplies. Another offered the use of his truck to haul supplies. Others volunteered similar help. Then Robert came forward. Robert is a quadriplegic who is confined to a motorized wheelchair and almost unable to speak. How could he go? What could he offer?

In halting, slurred speech, Robert told the group that he promised to pray for the team, individual by individual, until they returned. Each of the team members embraced Robert, tears blurring their vision.

Later, members of the team reported on their many difficulties. When they were most weary and most wanted to give up on their efforts, they remembered Robert. They knew he was praying for them at that very moment. Undergirded by a sense of those prayers, they found new strength and resolve to serve those whose homes had been destroyed.

Service takes many forms, none of more value than any other, and it involves us in the lives of many people.

Whom do we serve? It is easy to think of serving the suffering, the poor, the homeless, and the ill. But Christ demonstrated that we are to serve all of God's people. Consider how he served the wealthy (Nicodemus and Zacchaeus) and how he served the humble members of his immediate group (when he washed the feet of the apostles).

We often look beyond our immediate surroundings for someone to serve. And yet, there are many opportu-
nities to serve in our home congregations and communities. How to serve is another challenge. Does serving others mean giving them what they want and what they ask for? Look at Jesus. The Gospels are filled with stories of Jesus giving people something far greater than they recognized was needed.

The task of the servant is to provide others with what they need for life abundant. "For my thoughts are not your thoughts, nor are your ways my ways, says the LORD" (Isaiah 55:8). Simply acceding to the wishes of others is not always serving them in the best possible way.

Studies of addictions have demonstrated that giving people what they want may be destructive. For example, the word *enabler* has negative connotations in the treatment of addictions. An enabler is one who seeks to help but whose actions are, in fact, destructive. Thus, the spouse who regularly covers up a partner's addiction or the friend who continually loans money to the addict may be fostering the addictions.

The servant may be called to demonstrate tough love. To the woman taken in adultery, Jesus said, "Neither do I condemn you. Go your way, and from now on do not sin again" (John 8:11). Jesus served the woman by protecting her from the hostility of the mob and by offering her the forgiveness of God, but at the same time he did not condone her lifestyle. Serving is not simply saying, "I will do whatever you want."

Servanthood is perhaps best demonstrated by Jesus when he washed the feet of the apostles. Notice what Jesus did in this situation (John 13:1-20).

First, he served when his apostles least expected it. This was a night of celebration and joy; the apostles were having a special ritual dinner with their Lord. Their thoughts must have been far from ideas of service, sacrifice, and self-giving.

Second, Jesus served in a way that his apostles found most astonishing. Foot-washing was a common practice in first-century Judea, but it was always done by the lowliest servant. While Jesus could have served his brothers in a variety of ways, he went to the extreme, serving by humbling himself. He demonstrated that service means an absolute and total self-giving. (His crucifixion on the next day was the supreme example of giving one's self for others!)

Third, in washing the apostles' feet, Jesus demonstrated that all of us need to receive the service of others. At first Peter refused to allow Jesus to wash his feet. One of the most difficult things Peter had to do was to recognize his own needs and to allow another to minister to those needs. We, too, need to accept the gracious ministry of others. One of the truest ways we can serve is to allow another to serve us, graciously accepting the service with thanksgiving.

We hope your lay speaker group will decide to experience foot-washing. You may choose one of many modes, including the use of water and a basin. Or you may choose a symbolic ritual (wiping shoes with a towel), in order to avoid the initial anxiety some may feel or to avoid the difficulty of removing shoes and socks or hose. In either case, urge people to kneel (if possible) as they wash or wipe, demonstrating the servanthood of ministry done in Christ's name.

In some churches, a mild moisturizing lotion is distributed to the participants, and each participant experiences having her or his hands rubbed with the lotion by the person sitting next to her or him. One of us experienced this one evening in a small-membership rural church. As the lotion was distributed, one crusty old farmer muttered under his breath about how silly the whole thing was. He made it quite clear that he did not want to do this and simply wanted to be excused. But he could not. Protesting under his breath, he put a dab of lotion on his hand and turned to the person next to him. She was an elderly widow, who was also apprehensive. The group members focused their attention on performing the ritual. But, slowly, the room grew silent, and it was apparent that all were staring in the same direction—at the old farmer as he gently stroked the widow's cheeks with the lotion. Surely this was the first time in years that anyone had touched the older woman's face. Though her eyes were tightly closed and tears flowed down her cheeks, she was smiling and radiating joy. Beautiful as this was, it was even more beautiful to see the tears that welled up in the man's eyes and dripped off his chin as he discovered the simple joy of serving and being served.

To serve as Jesus served. To accept the love and ministry of others as Jesus did. To be lavishly loving in our self-giving service. To this we, as lay speakers, are called.

Called to Proclaim the Gospel Through Growing in Personal Faith

9

We have talked about the duties, the responsibilities, the possibilities, and the potential open to a lay speaker. You may be thinking that doing all of these—leading worship, preaching, teaching, serving, witnessing—is a tall order. And it is.

So, where and how do you find the impetus and the motivation? That is what this chapter is about: finding and using the resources that can help feed you spiritually. This is also known as growing in personal faith, walking more closely with the Lord day by day, and keeping anchored in your faith in Jesus Christ as Lord and Savior. The question is, How do you do it?

Here are our suggestions. Perhaps these, as is or modified, will work for you.

Awareness

Develop a sense of God-consciousness. Live every moment of your life aware of God's presence in your life. Be aware of God's presence with you wherever you are and whatever you are doing.

Breath prayers

The ancient monks of the Christian faith developed breath prayers. A breath prayer is a short phrase or prayer that is brief enough to be uttered each time you exhale a breath of air. Some examples are, "Be with me, Lord"; "Thank you, Lord"; "Lord, have mercy"; or some other simple phrase. The idea is to repeat this phrase so often (aloud, silently, even mentally) that it becomes almost automatic to send up a prayer with every breath. Thus, your breath prayer is your first conscious thought in the morning and your last conscious thought at night. A breath prayer sustains you throughout the day by ensuring you of God's continuing presence at each moment of the day.

Another form of the breath prayer is a longer phrase, repeated often during the day and used as a way to re-establish contact with God, to calm down, to get one's bearing, and to regain a sense of inner peace and control at a time of chaos. One of the classic longer breath prayers, "Lord Jesus Christ, Son of God, Savior of the world," is said or thought as a breath is inhaled; the last part, "have mercy on me," is said or thought as the breath is exhaled. Because the first phrase is relatively long and is said during inhaling, this breath prayer forces the user to inhale long and deeply, a boon to physical health as well as a way of reconnecting with God.

Journaling

Another way to maintain contact with God throughout the day is through the increasingly popular practice of spiritual journaling. Here, a person sets aside a certain time each day, maybe even two or three times each day, to write. A journal is not a diary; it is more than a what-happened-to-me-today account. A spiritual journal contains one's reflections on interactions with God. These may come through sight, sound, senses, or people, to name a few possibilities. Beyond that, there are no rules. Your journal can be a loose-leaf notebook, a tablet, a file in your computer, a stack of index cards, or even a tape recorder. Your journal is for no one's eyes but your own; it is not to be shared, discussed, described, or critiqued. It is simply a record of your sense of God's presence through the day. Some people are more disciplined in their journaling. One popular approach is to select a Scripture passage early in the morning, pray about that passage, and then spend the day thinking about and reflecting on the passage. Keep journal notes throughout the day as the passage comes to your mind. If you try this, keep the passages short, precise, to the point—perhaps a parable, a statement of Paul's, or some verses from a psalm.

One of us has kept a journal for years, filling several spiral wire-bound notebooks, each dated. The current journal goes with us wherever we go and is used daily. The journals and their contents are absolutely private and confidential. Only the writer and God know what is in them. With any style of journaling, this is a necessity.

Meditation

Several years ago, I attended a course in Bible interpretation where each student was given a short passage of Scripture, then asked to spend the rest of the day meditating on it. I was given the story of the feeding of the five thousand. I thought, *I know that story inside and out. What can I get out of thinking about a familiar story all day?* But, off I went, deciding to take a long walk in the fresh spring air. I wandered for hours along some country lanes, wondering what I was supposed to discover about this passage. Then, slowly, I began to experience the hunger of the people on that Galilean hillside more than two thousand years earlier. I began to sense and feel their thirst as they sat in the relentless sunshine listening to the Master. But I quickly realized my hunger and thirst were not physical but spiritual. I hungered for a deeper and closer walk with Jesus Christ, and for an even greater assurance that I was living my life the way God intended. I hungered for the assurance that God still knew me, loved me, and wanted me. Then I experienced Christ filling me with a sense of his presence, his peace, his love, and his power. As the people on that hillside went home from that experience with Christ filled and warmed, so did I return to the dormitory filled with a new awareness of how Jesus Christ meets the deep spiritual hungers in our lives.

Do you notice what it took for me to discover that sense of God's presence? It took time, a separation from the everydayness of life, and a willingness to concentrate, reflect, and meditate on a Scripture that God has given us. The time need not be all day; the separation need not be on a country road far from anyone else; and the concentration on Scripture need not come from a classroom assignment. The time, place, and motivation are as individual as you are. But give God these three, and discover what the presence of the Lord can do in and for you.

Intentional daily time

As significant as breath prayers, journaling, and meditations are, do not let them take the place of an intentional regular daily time spent with God in prayer, meditation, and study. You choose the time. An ancient Jewish legend says that early prayers are the best, so many Orthodox Jews rise before dawn to offer their prayers to God. But not all of us are early morning people (neither of us are), so do not be discouraged if you try early devotions and it just does not work for you. Find another time, and develop the absolute discipline that you will hold this time sacred no matter what.

A mutual friend of ours, now retired, was part of a Methodist Youth Fellowship group in the late 1940's. As these teens grew closer, they realized that their high school graduation was imminent, and they would not be together in the same way again. So, they made a covenant to pray for one another at ten P.M. each day, no matter where they were or what they were doing. Our friend still prays for each of his friends at ten P.M. We have been in social situations with him when, at the stroke of ten, he quietly excuses himself, finds a quiet place, and prays for his friends. He says the knowledge that his friends are also praying for him at the same time has sustained him through a lifetime of joys, sorrows, victories, and defeats.

Some people might say, "OK, I've set apart a time each day. What do I do?" The choice is yours. You might begin with an invocational prayer, a Bible reading and reflection, a devotional reading and reflection, and a personal prayer that ends, perhaps, with our Lord's Prayer or another suitable prayer.

You might use any of the excellent and easily available lists of daily Bible readings. (If your adult Sunday school class is using a version of the International Lesson Series, daily Bible readings accompany that.) The American Bible Society publishes a list of daily readings annually and also provides lists by which you can read the entire Bible through in a single year. These are helpful tools in Bible reading. But keep in mind that this is not Bible study—that comes at another time. What you are doing is letting the biblical text speak to you; you are allowing those words to wash over you and make you different than you have been before. Select short passages for reflection. Try to memorize some of what you reflect upon each day—perhaps a phrase or a line that you can take with you throughout the day. Here is a hint: Get a Bible with large type and wide margins so that you can underline, highlight, and make notes, questions, and comments. Make this Bible yours!

Allow a quiet time after reading the Scripture. Resist the urge to close the Bible and grab a devotional piece in the same motion. Read the biblical passage several times, savor it, then reflect on it in silence (or by journaling) for several minutes. Consider several perspectives.

Then turn to some devotional reading. *The Upper Room* is written by people just like you who have experienced God's presence and power in their lives. Some lay speakers use *Guideposts* or any of several other popular devotional magazines. Three books published by Upper Room Books continue to grow in popularity and use: *A Guide to Prayer for Ministers and Other Servants*, *A Guide to Prayer for All God's People,* and *A Guide to Prayer for All Who Seek God*. Since these call on the wisdom of the centuries, they are gold mines of inspiration, challenge, and insight. Do not forget *The United Methodist Hymnal*. From time to time read (not sing) the words of a hymn. Reflect on the words and their message and meaning for you. What was the writer trying to communicate through these words, and how are you experiencing the same presence of God that the writer describes in the poetry of the hymn?

Again, allow time to reflect, to saturate yourself in thoughts of what God is trying to communicate to and through you for this day; then move on to prayer. Let your prayer be one of thanksgiving and praise, a prayer of confession, a prayer of intercession in which you pray for others, a prayer of supplication in which you pray for yourself, and a prayer of commitment in which you promise yourself as you promise God that you will in every way seek to live this day in God's will.

How long should daily devotions take? Your time with the Lord cannot be determined by a clock or a formula. Start with a comparatively brief time; chances are this time will increase. Perhaps our personal devotions are a little like eating a fine meal: Doctors counsel us to stop eating when we are still just a bit hungry. If we end our personal devotional each day wanting just a bit more, we will take that hunger throughout the day and find ourselves reflecting even more on the presence of God.

We have been asked, "Do you ever get to the point where you do not need this quiet time each day?" The obvious response is, "Did Jesus?" The Gospels show that Jesus repeatedly went off alone to be in dialogue with God. If Jesus Christ, God incarnate, needed this quiet time each day, so do we!

A final word: We have all heard the cliché about the plumber's home having leaky faucets. We can err in this way also. Our private daily devotions are centrally important; yet, we must make time each day to spend in prayer and reflection with our families. Even among the most hectic of family schedules, strive to find some time each day when you, as a family, can reflect on what God is doing in your life. Be faithful even if not all family members can be present each time. A brief Bible reading, a devotional piece, and a time of family prayer in which each member is invited to pray can constitute your family devotional time. Again, regularity is the key. As one family put it, "This is just what we do; it's as much a part of our mealtime as having a beverage with our food."

In the busyness of being a lay speaker, neglecting our own spiritual growth is a constant temptation. But we can be only as effective in our Lay Speaking Ministries as we are in daily contact with God.

Called to Proclaim the Gospel Through a Personal Lifestyle

10

At vacation Bible school one year, the youngsters sang a lively song called "Walk, Walk Your Talk!" They sang it with clever motions and gestures, the boys popping up in the back rows singing, "Walk, walk your talk" as the girls in the front rows sang the verses.

When the children sang the song for the parents, they loved it and gave it a loud ovation. But the point of the song was not lost in the energized rendition: We are indeed called to practice what we preach, to realize that actions speak more loudly than words. Clearly, it is not enough to be just a professing Christian. We must reflect the presence of Jesus Christ daily, not just when we are performing a liturgical duty or acting as a lay speaker, but in every place and in every deed. We are talking about a Christian lifestyle. Walk the talk!

A definition

A Christian lifestyle is a way of living every moment of our lives with Jesus Christ at the very center. It is easy to say but difficult to do. We cannot put Christ at the very center without denying ourselves, putting aside some of our own inclinations and desires. For example, many of us say with passion, "Family comes first with me!" Yet, is that actually reflected in our lives? We attended a business seminar several years ago where we were asked to list the amount of time we spend on the activities in our lives—job, recreation, relaxation, preparation for work, family, and so on. Most of us ranked our families as our most important priority; but in terms of actual time spent with the family, our families came in a distant fifth or sixth, behind such things as job, professional development, and so on.

As important as our family is, it cannot be the center of our lives. Jesus Christ must occupy that position. Jesus made harsh comments about people putting family ahead of the kingdom of God. This was done to help us realize that we are able to love our family more genuinely with a Christlike love. Putting Christ first enables us to do that far more effectively and selflessly than ever before.

A Christian lifestyle is one that sees each person as a sister or brother in Christ. It is a lifestyle in which prejudices, generalizations, stereotypes, and labels disappear. We are freed, by the grace of God, to see each person as a unique child of God who is loved, sustained, and redeemed by God and is worthy of a place in eternity. People of all races and nationalities, all socioeconomic and educational levels, and all geographic areas will greet us when we come into eternity with Christ.

What would it mean for you as a lay speaker to meet the most ordinary of people as a brother or sister in Christ? Think about that this week. Who in your daily activity do you take for granted the most? the shuffling homeless person? the seemingly able-bodied fellow on the street corner who holds the sign "Will work for food"? the bus driver? the person working the checkout counter at the supermarket? the faceless crew that picks up your trash or the unseen person who delivers your morning newspaper long before you even get up? Ask yourself: *If I were to begin seeing and treating this person as a sister or brother in Christ, what would I do differently? If I were to perceive this person as of inestimable worth (worth Jesus Christ dying on a cross) and to recognize my own sinful, frightened, lonely, and anxious self in this person, how would I treat this person differently?* A Christian lifestyle demands that we see each person as a brother or sister in Christ. Beside that basic characteristic, all of our artificial distinctions pale into nothingness.

Peter struggled over whether the message of salvation was for Jews only or for all people, until God sent him the vision of the sheet filled with food (see Acts 11:1-18). Jesus never grappled with the issue; he simply loved the Samaritan, the tax collector, the woman taken in adultery, the blind beggar, the unclean woman with the flow of blood, the thief on the cross. If we choose to live a Christian lifestyle—and we must if we are to belong to Jesus Christ—then we must love and serve without exception and as freely and as openly as he did.

A Christian lifestyle is one in which values, decisions, and choices reflect the presence of Christ. Some decisions are clearly right or wrong, clearly in accord with the way of Christ or clearly contrary to the will of Christ. These are easy. The same is true with values. As members of the body of Christ, we value certain characteristics, attributes, ways of living; we disvalue others that are discordant to the body of Christ. Ananias and Sapphira demonstrated selfishness and greed, clearly violating Christian values (Acts 5:1-11).

But what about all of those values and decisions that are not clear and obvious—those over which Christians can and do differ, or areas where equally committed Christians see the same issue from different perspectives and arrive at different responses or actions? How do we know what is the will of God?

As a denomination, The United Methodist Church helps with that through the Social Principles. They are issued by the General Conference every four years and published in *The Book of Discipline of The United Methodist Church*. The Social Principles list the church's stance on some of the great issues facing our families, our communities, our nation, and our world. We may not all agree with each one, but we must acknowledge that the General Conference, the only group that can speak for our denomination, has prayerfully and carefully considered the issues, sought to determine the will of God in each, and stated where we stand as a denomination.

You will find the Social Principles in either the *Book of Discipline* or the pamphlet edition, both available through Cokesbury. You will note that some of the statements in the Social Principles are not absolute; Christians still struggle with many difficult issues. But the Social Principles seek to lift the issues involved and the way of Christ as revealed in the Gospels, helping these intersect as much as possible. Some issues are not mentioned in the Social Principles; these are issues on which the church has not chosen to speak or around which uncertainty about the most appropriate Christian response is still prevalent.

By the way, what if you disagree with a position the church has taken in the Social Principles? Are you automatically out of the church? Of course not! But you can influence where the church stands on major social issues by submitting a petition to the General Conference or by contacting your congregation's annual conference delegate and expressing your views. This does not guarantee a change in position, but the denomination is eager to hear from all of its members about the stances the church has adopted. Your ideas and input are important.

Reaching conclusions about emerging issues

Issues will arise when the church has not spoken definitively on a matter. How does the Christian reach decisions in these instances? What questions should the Christian ask?

Some questions to consider are

- Who wins and who loses by each possible choice of action? Is a way available to make everybody win?
- Which choice will most nearly glorify God?
- Which choice affirms the dignity and God-createdness of the people involved most directly?
- What motives drive the possibilities?
- What are the long-term effects?
- Ultimately, the question "What would Jesus do?" should guide us.

Finally, we must subjugate the self and focus on Christ. With that, we may still differ, but we respect our differences because they are Christ-centered, not self-centered.

A Christian lifestyle is one of joy and gladness. Paul said, "Give thanks in all circumstances" (1 Thessalonians 5:18a). A Christian knows that she or he is in possession of the greatest gift: the gospel of Jesus Christ. Owning this, how can we go through life angry, anxious, or complaining?

This does not mean that the Christian laughs off troubles (or that the Christian has no troubles). Instead, the Christian knows that God is with us through our troubles.

The Christian has the quiet joy and confidence of knowing that God is in control, that God has not stopped loving us, and that we can confidently affirm to one another: God loves you and cares about you! Christian joy is not necessarily laughter and gaiety at all times, but it is the quiet confidence of living a life of thanksgiving to a God who makes all things new.

And a Christian lifestyle is a lifestyle of hope. Hope is not a Christmas wish list or an empty longing for something far away and practically impossible. Christian hope is the confidence that we shall one day fully claim God's promises that are made through Jesus Christ and revealed in the Scriptures. Walk the talk! As lay speakers, we can talk a lot about our Christian faith. We can recite our beliefs. We can quote Scripture and discuss the details of Wesley's theology. We can practice all kinds of spiritual disciplines and set aside an hour each day for personal devotions. But, unless our daily walk reflects our faith, unless others can see Christ in our lives wherever we are or whatever we are doing, unless what we do matches and, indeed, exceeds what we say, then we are surely nothing more than "noisy gongs and clanging cymbals."

In Conclusion and Covenant

God has called you. God has called you to proclaim the gospel of Jesus Christ. God has called you to witness to your faith in the midst of a world that questions, doubts, and even (at times) ridicules.

God has called you to live out your faith in such a way that others will see the reflection of Jesus Christ in you. God has called you to teach, to lead, to follow, and to be a disciple.

God has called you. And you have answered.

Your answer may have been tentative. Even now, as you come to the final portion of this manual, you may have some doubts. You may wonder if it is really God who is calling. You may wonder if you can live up to the responsibility and opportunity as a lay speaker in The United Methodist Church. You may wonder if you are qualified, if you are capable, if you are good enough.

The answer comes as part of the call from God: No, not by yourself.

However, by trusting in God and God's presence, you are more than qualified, more than good enough, more than ready, and more than equipped! Thanks be to God; it is God's grace and not our own skill that makes the difference. Thanks be to God; it is God's presence with us and not our own abilities that makes us effective.

Because you have responded, God will fulfill God's part of the covenant. God has promised you that God knows you by name; it is by that name that God has called you. God has promised that God will give you the words to speak and the responses to make if you are open to the coaching and the direction of God.

God has promised that God will be with you, even unto the end of the world, if you go to proclaim the gospel of Jesus Christ. And God has promised, through the ringing words of Romans 8:38-39, "that neither death, nor life, nor angels, nor rulers, nor things present, nor things to come, nor powers, nor height, nor depth, nor anything else in all creation, will be able to separate us from the love of God in Christ Jesus our Lord."

Now, lead a committee, step up to a pulpit, visit a prison, teach a Bible class, work as a member of a task force—secure in the promises of God for you, for all of the people of God, and for the congregation you are seeking to serve.

A caution

Saying yes to God's call does not exclude us from the trials of life. You may be misinterpreted, criticized, and discouraged. Be encouraged by the many who have remained faithful, including Paul, Martin Luther, Albert Schweitzer, and even Jesus Christ himself. The prayer below comes from Wesley's Covenant Service, a service frequently conducted on New Year's Eve but appropriate at any time. Read it silently, then aloud. Then, if you can, offer this prayer to God as your promise and your commitment:

I am no longer my own, but thine.
Put me to what thou wilt, rank me with whom
*   thou wilt.*
Put me to doing, put me to suffering.
Let me be employed by thee or laid aside
*   for thee,*
exalted for thee or brought low for thee.
Let me be full, let me be empty.
Let me have all things, let me have nothing.
I freely and heartily yield all things
to thy pleasure and disposal.
And now, O glorious and blessed God,
Father, Son, and Holy Spirit,
thou art mine, and I am thine. So be it.
And the covenant which I have made on earth,
let it be ratified in heaven. Amen.

("A Covenant Prayer in the Wesleyan Tradition," in *The United Methodist Hymnal,* 607.)

Leader's Guide

Welcome to a spiritual journey, one of reading and reflection, journaling and dialogue, and discovery and direction. With God as your guide, you will be traveling with the enthusiastic and eager individuals who have come to examine God's call on their lives through Lay Speaking Ministries.

GENERAL INFORMATION

1. Scheduling

The text is divided into eleven chapters, all based on the theme "Called to Proclaim the Gospel." The training model assumes at least ten contact hours, but in scheduling your sessions, we urge you to (a) allow for sufficient preparation time between sessions, and (b) increase the length of the sessions (from sixty minutes to seventy-five minutes, from two hours to two and a half hours, and so forth). Caution: Do not let yourself be so bound by the clock that you detract from the experience!

If you are using the weekend format of Friday night and Saturday, consider extending the course into Saturday night. Better yet, finish on Sunday morning and close with a worship service.

If you are scheduling ten separate sessions, you may adapt the *Leader's Guide* by dividing the session plan at the break. If you use this model, be sure to give the assignment for the next session.

2. Preparation

The *Lay Speaking Ministries: Basic Course* presupposes outside preparation by each participant, including completion of all assignments before the first session (Chapter 1). Preparation includes reading the chapter, reflecting on the material, and completing the appropriate activities and biblical assignments. Class time is frequently based on the prepared assignments.

3. Commitment

The course presupposes commitment to faithful attendance and full participation. Absentees and dropouts will negatively affect all group members. Lead the participants in making a covenant for faithful attendance and full participation.

4. Interaction

The course is designed for discussion, conversation, sharing, practicing, and experiencing. As a leader, you are not expected or encouraged to make extensive formal presentations or to give lectures. Do not yield to temptation!

5. Hospitality

Set the tone for hospitality! Prepare the room with tables and chairs (you will need workspace to spread out, and tables are required for many of the activities), newsprint, markers, additional Bibles, hymnals, and other references. Use nametags for the first session (at least), and provide lists of the participants' addresses after the roster is finalized. Consider providing beverages and light refreshments at breaks if your sessions last longer than two hours. Gently encourage people to sit in different locations at each session and after breaks to encourage more interaction.

6. Leader participation

Be a full participant as well as the leader; participate in all of the assignments, conversations, and reflections. Share your spiritual pilgrimage as participants share with you.

7. Timekeeping

Once your course times are set, be deliberate about both starting and ending on time. Do not give permission to come late by always starting late. And be sensitive to commitments after the session by always ending at the agreed time.

In addition, be a timekeeper. Although you and your participants may want to stay with one issue or activity, move the group to complete the content of the session. When interest is particularly high on a topic, arrange for after-session conversations.

8. Basic tools

Each participant, including you, will need a copy of this manual, a Bible, and a notebook for reflective writing.

9. Resources

Basic resources that each participant will need (or need access to) are *The United Methodist Hymnal*, *The United Methodist Book of Worship* (at a minimum, have one copy for each three participants), *The Book of Discipline of The United Methodist Church—2004*, and the pamphlet edition of the *Social Principles of The United Methodist Church—2004* (available through Cokesbury).

Session One: Called by God

The main purposes of this session are

- to explore the nature and meaning of a call from God;
- to develop an understanding of United Methodist theology.

Participant preparation
- Read Chapters 1 and 2, pages 1–5 in this manual.
- Complete at least Activities 1 and 2 on page 2.

Supplies and resources
- The United Methodist *Discipline*
- *The United Methodist Hymnal*
- *Lay Speaking Ministries: Basic Course*
- Bibles
- Bible concordances
- Nametags
- Newsprint and felt-tip markers
- Masking tape
- Participant journals
- Pens or pencils

Outline

Part 1: Called by God
1. Welcome, opening prayer, brief description of Lay Speaking Ministries (10 minutes)
2. Introductions and get-acquainted activity (10 minutes)
3. Bible study: People of the Bible who experienced God's call (18 minutes)
4. God's call to people of today: Relating interviews (9 minutes)
5. Personal experiences of God's call: Journaling (8 minutes)

   STRETCH BREAK (5 minutes)

Part 2: Called to proclaim the gospel
6. United Methodist doctrinal heritage (20 minutes)
7. Using the *Discipline*: Our beliefs (20 minutes)
8. Examining the Social Principles (17 minutes)
9. Assignments and closing (8 minutes)

TOTAL TIME: 2 hours, 5 minutes

SESSION PLAN

1. Begin the session with prayer, praying for God's presence and guidance for each participant as she or he seeks to discern God's call to lay speaking. Welcome all participants, being sure that each has both a copy of this manual *(Lay Speaking Ministries: Basic Course)* and a Bible. Briefly describe the lay speaking program, including the differences between local church lay speakers and those certified through advanced study. (See the *Book of Discipline* for information on the differences.) Describe the kinds of witnessing opportunities that each participant might expect as a lay speaker. Remind the participants of the expectations for preparation and attendance, and then lead them in a prayer of covenant.

2. Direct each person to turn to another person and introduce herself or himself (name, home church, role in the church). Ask each person to tell his or her partner how he or she came to attend this lay speaker training. Then ask the partners to introduce each other to the larger group. (Note: If your group includes more than twelve participants, do the introductions in table groups or other smaller groups.)

3. List on newsprint the names of biblical characters cited on page 1 who experienced God's call (Moses, Mary, Esther, Saul, Samuel, Martha, Gideon, Sarah, Amos, Jeremiah, Elijah, Peter, James, John, Matthew, Zacchaeus, Abraham, Jacob, the Gentile foreigner on the road to Gaza, the harlot at a well in Samaria, the Canaanite woman, and the thief hanging on a cross).

   Divide into groups of three and assign each group three biblical people to participants. Ask each triad to (a) locate the biblical reference, (b) learn about the character, and (c) describe the character's call.

   (This may be an opportunity to describe the use of the concordance and name index found in many Bibles. You may decide to provide additional concordances.)

   Next, ask group members to report their findings. Guide discussion about the ways God calls and the ways people respond.

4. Send the participants back to their triads to discuss findings from interviews they did in preparation for this first session (activity 2, on page 2). Ask them to consider the following: How did God call the person? What was the initial response? the later response? How is his or her call like a biblical character's?

5. Direct the participants to write in their journal about their own call to ministry and to lay speaking and about what they are learning about the call of God.

STRETCH BREAK

6. Divide participants into three groups. Give each group a large sheet of newsprint and a marker. Be sure there is a copy of *The Book of Discipline* in each group. Assign each group the task of summarizing a part of the information in Chapter 2 on pages 4–5. Group 1 will summarize the common core of Christian beliefs, called "Basic Christian Affirmations" in the *Discipline*. Group 2 will summarize our United Methodist theological heritage, including the "Distinctive Wesleyan Emphases" named in the *Discipline*. Group 3 will summarize the United Methodist understanding of our theological task, including the four tools United Methodists use to "do theology." Tape their newsprint sheets together in one place and ask each group to comment on what they have found.

7. Divide the group into pairs. Give each pair a copy of the current *Book of Discipline*. Remind them that, through the action of our quadrennial General Conference, the *Discipline* is the authoritative voice for our denomination. Then assign the pairs words or phrases (*marriage, divorce, the family, rights of children, genetic technology, gambling, military service, abortion,* or others from the Social Principles) and have them answer these questions: What does The United Methodist Church believe about __? Is this belief part of the common core of Christian beliefs; a distinctive United Methodist belief; or reached through the "Wesleyan quadri-lateral" of Scripture, tradition, experience, and reason? (Many will be part of all three.)

8. Based on our understandings of Scripture and our theological beliefs, The United Methodist Church through the General Conference makes statements about social issues. Many of these are controversial, and may not be affirmed by all lay speakers. As you present these to the participants, stress the process by which the statements are reached, the way individuals and churches can effect changes every four years, and the responsibility of lay speakers to present faithfully the official statements of the church. List on newsprint the first six sections within the Social Principles ("The Natural World," "The Nurturing Community," "The Social Community," "The Economic Community," "The Political Community," and "The World Community"). Then divide the participants into six teams, assigning one section per team. Ask each team to cite the issues presented in their assigned section and to consider statements with which they most agree and statements with which they most disagree.

9. Make the following assignments:

   • Read Luke 4:14-41; Acts 2:14-42.
   • Read Chapters 3 and 4 in this manual.
   • Examine "The Basic Pattern of Worship" (*The United Methodist Hymnal*, page 2). Compare it with the worship bulletin at your church.
   • Become familiar with divisions found in the *Hymnal*. Look particularly for liturgical seasons, prayers, responsive readings, indexes, and groupings of hymns.
   • Assign one person to begin the next session by leading the group in a brief meditation based on the Lectionary Scriptures.

Have the participants gather in a circle. Remind the group that, as a connectional church, we are bound to each other through both faith and polity. Sing as a prayer "Blest Be the Tie That Binds" (*Hymnal*, 557).

Session Two: Called to Lead Worship

The main purposes of this session are

- to understand the role of the lay speaker as a leader in worship;
- to develop a working knowledge of the liturgical calendar and other resources for worship preparation, including *The United Methodist Hymnal* and *The United Methodist Book of Worship*;
- to understand that each element of worship must be focused toward a cohesive theme, must draw the worshipers toward God in Jesus Christ, and should move them toward a response of discipleship;
- to learn how to prepare a sermon, including choosing Scripture, developing themes, using liturgical guides, practicing, and evaluating.

The work done in this session is the foundation for the short preaching assignments throughout the rest of the course.

Supplies and resources
- *The United Methodist Book of Worship*
- *The United Methodist Hymnal*
- *Lay Speaking Ministries: Basic Course*
- Bibles
- Newsprint
- Felt-tip markers
- Masking tape
- Participant journals
- Pens or pencils
- White, red, green, and purple construction paper

Outline

Part 1: Called to proclaim the gospel through worship leadership
1. Welcome, meditation, and prayer (13 minutes)
2. Remembering worship services (6 minutes)
3. The basic outline of a worship service (14 minutes)
4. Selecting hymns (12 minutes)
5. Examining the Christian year (20 minutes)
6. Reflection (5 minutes)

STRETCH BREAK (5 minutes)

Part 2: Called to proclaim the gospel through preaching
7. Analyzing preaching (9 minutes)
8. Reflection (3 minutes)
9. Examining the Lectionary (25 minutes)
10. Preparing to preach (15 minutes)
11. Assignments and closing (8 minutes)

TOTAL TIME: 2 hours, 15 minutes

SESSION PLAN

1. Welcome the participants and encourage them to sit in a different place than where they sat last session. Review the emphases of this session by listing them on newsprint. Let the assigned person lead the meditation.

2. Ask the participants to recall and make notes about the best worship service they ever attended, using the following questions:

   - Where was it?
   - When was it?
   - What was your role: congregational participant, choir member, liturgist, acolyte?
   - What made it memorable?

   Note that each person will define "best" differently. Ask the participants to use the same questions to reflect on the most disappointing worship service they ever attended.

   Divide the participants into groups of three; then ask them to discuss their memories about both the best and the most disappointing worship services.

3. Examine together "The Basic Pattern of Worship" (*The United Methodist Hymnal*, page 2). Identify the four sections noted in Chapter 3 in this manual: Entrance, Proclamation and Response, Thanksgiving and Communion, and Sending Forth. Discuss the rationale for the placement of the message and offering. Then walk through "An Order of Sunday Worship" (*Hymnal*, pages 3–5), noting the suggested prayers, readings, and other acts of worship. As you discuss the sacraments, you will want to state clearly that only licensed local pastors and ordained clergy are authorized to serve

the sacrament of Holy Communion in The United Methodist Church.

4. After pointing out the "Index of Topics and Categories" (Hymnal, pages 934–54), assign table groups to select hymns appropriate for each of the four parts of worship during the current season of the church year. Post four sheets of newsprint, each labeled with one of the parts of worship, around the room. Ask the table groups to list their selected hymns on the appropriate pages.

5. Give each table group sheets of colored construction paper (white, red, green, and purple) with the following labels at the top of the sheets:

   • Advent (purple paper)
   • Christmas Season (white paper)
   • Christmas Day (white paper)
   • Epiphany of the Lord (white paper)
   • Season After Epiphany (green paper)
   • Baptism of the Lord (white paper)
   • Lent (purple paper)
   • Ash Wednesday (purple paper)
   • Holy Thursday (purple paper)
   • Easter Season (white paper)
   • Easter Day (white paper)
   • Day of Pentecost (red paper)
   • Season After Pentecost (green paper)
   • All Saints Day (white paper)

   Ask the table groups to list on newsprint as much information as possible about each season or day, including suggested invocations, prayers of confession, hymns, and so forth. Make sure each group has copies of The United Methodist Hymnal and The United Methodist Book of Worship to use as references. Have the participants post the newsprint sheets on the wall, and encourage them to look during the break at what other groups have done. (The participants may want to compile the results of this exercise into a reference booklet to use in the future when they are asked to lead worship.)

6. Direct the participants, using their journals, to reflect on what they have learned about worship planning and preparation. Also urge them to note specific resources for later referral.

STRETCH BREAK

7. Divide into groups of three people and give each group two sheets of newsprint with the written headings "Good preaching includes . . ." and "Poor preaching includes . . ." Urge them to list as many responses as possible. Then have them compare and discuss the lists with two other triads. As a whole group, discuss common emerging themes.

8. Ask the participants to reflect silently on God's leading them to occasional preaching as lay speakers in The United Methodist Church.

9. Introduce the Revised Common Lectionary (see the Book of Worship, pages 227–37). With the group, identify the four Scriptures for the next Sunday. Then divide participants into pairs. Each pair will study all four texts, considering these six questions for each one:

   • What is this about?
     (Check other translations.)
   • What precedes these verses?
   • What follows these verses?
   • What is the setting?
   • What insights can be gained from footnotes? commentaries? Bible dictionaries?
   • What questions does this passage raise?

   After they study each passage individually, direct the pairs to consider how the four passages interrelate.

   Then direct the pairs to decide on a point of good news for a hypothetical sermon and on three ways they would integrate the four Lectionary readings in making that point.

10. Ask each participant to study the Lectionary readings for Year A for the Sunday nearest to his or her birthday. Have them examine the Scriptures and resources and identify a point for preaching, making notes about possible directions. Then have them turn to a new partner, and have the partners discuss their texts and points, giving opportunities for feedback and clarification.

11. Make the following assignments:

    • Review Chapter 4 in this manual.
    • Prepare a five-minute meditation (think of it as a mini-sermon), using one or more of the Lectionary texts studied in exercise 10, to present to a small group at the next session.
    • Read Chapters 5 and 6 in this manual.

    Close by reading Jesus' words from Luke 4:18-19, asking the group members to repeat aloud each line after you. Give a benediction and blessing from the Book of Worship (559–67).

Session Three:
Called to Witness and Teach

3

The main purposes of this session are

- to provide a laboratory preaching experience through preparing, presenting, and receiving feedback;
- to explore the opportunities for witnessing and teaching as a lay speaker;
- to examine effective teaching techniques and styles.

You will want to set a tone of mutual caring and encouragement as the participants react to each others' presentations.

Supplies and resources

- *The United Methodist Book of Worship*
- *The United Methodist Hymnal*
- *Lay Speaking Ministries: Basic Course*
- Bibles
- Bible concordances or other Bible study aids
- Newsprint
- Felt-tip markers
- Masking tape
- Participant journals
- Pens or pencils
- Curriculum resources display

Outline

Part 1: Called to proclaim the gospel through witnessing
1. Welcome and prayer (3 minutes)
2. Preaching experiences (25 minutes)
3. Reflection (5 minutes)
4. Bible study (10 minutes)
5. Components of a positive witness (8 minutes)
6. Roleplays (12 minutes)
7. Reflection (3 minutes)

STRETCH BREAK (5 minutes)

Part 2: Called to proclaim the gospel through teaching
8. Recalling Sunday school (5 minutes)
9. Describing good teaching (8 minutes)
10. Teaching versus preaching (9 minutes)
11. Presentation: Faith and facts (15 minutes)
12. Examination of resources (12 minutes)
13. Reflection (5 minutes)
14. Assignments and closing (10 minutes)

TOTAL TIME: 2 hours, 15 minutes

SESSION PLAN

1. Welcome the participants and open with a prayer from the *Hymnal* or the *Book of Worship*.

2. Before the participants give their mini-sermons, present these criteria for providing feedback, and then post this list where all can see.

   Criteria: Did the speaker

   - have something to say? Did she or he say it?
   - stay true to the scriptural text?
   - have smooth delivery?
   - have rapport with listeners?
   - grasp and hold the attention of the listeners?
   - show organization of ideas?
   - maintain eye contact?
   - use appropriate gestures and expressions?
   - keep to the allotted time?
   - make one clear point?
   - call listeners to respond?

   Divide the participants into groups of three, assigning each person to present her or his mini-sermon to the other two people in the triad. The triads are to provide honest feedback to each of the mini-sermons. Remind everyone to encourage the others with helpful comments and suggestions. Ask the triads to allow five minutes for each presentation and two minutes for feedback on each presentation.

3. Following the preaching presentations, direct the participants to pause for individual reflection on the experience and the feedback received. Ask them to write their reflections in their journals.

4. Using Bible concordances and other Bible study aids, have the participants work in table groups to search for biblical references to witnessing (stories or individual verses). In addition, have the table groups note characteristics about the witnessing itself. For example, in Acts 9:10-19, Ananias witnessed through his obedience, his representing Christ to Saul, and his presence with Saul.

5. List together on newsprint the components of a positive witnessing experience. What must such an experience include? What might it include?

6. Assign each table group a scenario for roleplaying. Give them a few minutes to assign roles and to prepare. After each presentation, give the group time to make both positive comments (be sure to get those first) and suggestions.

   Scenarios might include a hospital visit, a home visit to a first-time church visitor, a visit to a disgruntled church member, a conversation with another parent at a ball field, a visit with a family waiting during the surgery of a loved one, a welcome visit to a neighbor, and a conversation with a coworker about scriptural interpretation. You may want to create your own scenarios.

7. Direct the participants to reflect silently on their witness and future responses to witnessing opportunities by writing in their journals.

STRETCH BREAK

8. Ask the participants to form pairs and to recall and tell a memory from their Sunday school experience. How has this affected their lives?

9. Direct the participants, in table groups, to identify and list the characteristics of good teaching.

10. Ask the table groups to continue working together by discussing and listing the similarities and differences between preaching and teaching.

11. Briefly present the concepts of teaching for facts and teaching for faith. Teaching for facts is based on giving and receiving information. The teacher is perceived as the source and the students as the receivers. Mastery of facts, dates, and historical data is the goal. This is sometimes called teaching for information. Part of our religious education includes this model—for instance, when we learn the books of the Bible, the names of the disciples, or the number of plagues.

   Teaching for faith is the second model. The goal of teaching for faith is to transform individuals as they grow into more-Christlike disciples. The teacher is a guide rather than a source of information, and students contribute to the teacher's growth as the teacher leads them. Teaching for faith presents the biblical foundation and then calls people to respond based on their love for God and desire to serve faithfully. Teaching for faith is often called transformational teaching.

   Direct the participants to form pairs and to choose a familiar Bible story. Ask them to describe how to teach this story for facts, and then how to teach the same story for faith.

12. Procure and display curriculum resources from your district office, your Cokesbury Action Team representative, or from the local Cokesbury bookstore. Direct the participants to browse and then select one resource to examine more carefully. Ask them to tell others at their table what they have discovered about this resource (based on the following questions):

    - What is its theme?
    - What age level is it intended for?
    - How is the Bible used?
    - How easy is it to use the resource?
    - What teacher helps are provided?
    - What teaching model is used, teaching for facts or teaching for faith?
    - In what setting could you use this resource?

13. Direct the participants to reflect in their journals about how today's experience and learnings about teaching will influence their teaching in the future.

14. Make the following assignments:

    - Read Chapters 7 and 8 in this manual.
    - Prepare another five-minute mini-sermon to present to a small group at the next session, using the Lectionary Scripture(s) for Year B and for the Sunday nearest to the participant's mother's birthday. Remind them of the criteria used at today's session and the feedback they received.

    Close by reading together (as a prayer) the text of "How Shall They Hear the Word of God" (*Hymnal*, 649).

Session Four: Called to Leadership and Service

4

The main purposes of this session are

- to provide a laboratory preaching experience through preparing, presenting, and receiving feedback;
- to reflect on the ways Christ is proclaimed through leadership and service.

You will want to set the tone of mutual caring and encouragement, coupled with helpful evaluative comments and suggestions. Your role will include keeping watch on the time: It will be easy for the speaking and evaluating to absorb most of the session. Do not let it!

Supplies and resources
- *The United Methodist Book of Worship*
- *The United Methodist Hymnal*
- *Lay Speaking Ministries: Basic Course*
- Bibles
- Bible concordances and other Bible study aids
- Newsprint
- Felt-tip markers
- Masking tape
- Participant journals
- Pens or pencils

Outline

Part 1: Called to proclaim the gospel through leadership
1. Welcome and prayer (3 minutes)
2. Preaching experiences (25 minutes)
3. Reflection (5 minutes)
4. Bible study (20 minutes)
5. Sentence stems and reflection (14 minutes)

STRETCH BREAK (5 minutes)

Part 2: Called to proclaim the gospel through service
6. Bible study (15 minutes)
7. Identifying service in action (12 minutes)
8. Foot-washing (16 minutes)
9. Reflection (12 minutes)
10. Assignments and closing (10 minutes)

TOTAL TIME: 2 hours, 17 minutes

SESSION PLAN

1. Welcome the participants and open with a prayer from *The United Methodist Hymnal* or the *Book of Worship.*

2. Divide the participants into new groups of three (not the same groups as the last session). Review the criteria for the mini-sermons as well as the guidelines about caring evaluation and encouraging comments. Quickly send the participants to small groups, reminding them to keep careful watch on the time (five minutes for presentation, two minutes for feedback).

3. Following the preaching exercise, direct all the participants to spend time reflecting individually in their journals about the experience of preparing and presenting their message and about the feedback they received today. Encourage them to include what worked best and insights for improvement.

4. Invite each participant to identify two of her or his favorite leaders in the Bible (other than Jesus Christ). Consider these questions:

   - How did he or she proclaim the gospel (if New Testament) or proclaim God's will (if Old Testament) as well as lead people?
   - What characteristics distinguish these leaders as men or women of God? (8 minutes)

   In table groups, describe and discuss these leaders. (6 minutes)

   Invite the whole group to read aloud 1 Corinthians 13 (even though the participants may use several translations). As you read, direct the participants to listen for the ways love and leadership intersect. List those ways together as a large group. (6 minutes)

5. Divide each table into two groups. Give one group the sentence stem "A leader proclaiming the gospel through her or his leadership will ..." and the other group the sentence stem "A leader proclaiming the gospel through her or his leadership will not ..." Invite each group to list on newsprint as many different endings as they can.

Post the newsprint for all to see. Conclude this activity by directing the participants to reflect in their journals about their own approach to leadership and leadership as proclamation of the gospel.

STRETCH BREAK

6. Assign each table group one biblical character who proclaimed the gospel by serving. You may choose from Ananias, Lydia, the boy who offered his lunch, Martha, Joseph of Arimathea, or others you suggest. (Assign a character without giving the biblical reference so that the participants will experience using a concordance or biblical index.) Direct members of each table group to read the story silently, then to discuss as a group the ways the character served and witnessed for Christ. Then instruct them to identify another biblical person who proclaimed Christ through service in similar ways.

7. Lead the participants in a mental walk through their churches to identify invisible service performed by others within their congregations. Direct the participants to close their eyes; then take them inside the front door and have them look at the entry for signs of service. (This may include cleanliness, an attractive bulletin board, a list of donors, flowers, and so forth.) Continue to guide the participants in their mental tour of their churches.

When completed, ask people to list silently all the evidences of service they saw and to name, if possible, the servants responsible. Then ask the participants to discuss those lists with one other person using the following questions:

- How many examples of service did you identify?
- Were there any surprises?
- What did these instances of service reveal about the church?
- In what ways did they proclaim the gospel?

8. Have one participant (ask in advance) read aloud the story of Jesus washing the disciples' feet (John 13:3-17). The listeners should imagine themselves as one of the disciples. Then distribute paper towels to each table group and invite the participants to wipe the shoes of the others at the table. As this occurs, you or someone with musical ability can lead in singing familiar hymns and choruses.

9. Ask the participants to reflect silently in their journals on the experience of the symbolic foot-washing, focusing on these questions (which you may want to put on newsprint):

- What do you think the disciples thought and felt as Jesus moved around the room washing their feet?
- How did you react to wiping another's shoes?
- How did you react to having someone wipe your shoes?
- How do you receive service from others?
- What have you learned about proclaiming through service?

10. Make the following assignment:

- Read Chapters 9, 10, and 11 in the manual.
- Prepare a third five-minute mini-sermon to present to a small group at the next session, using the Lectionary Scriptures for Year C and for the Sunday nearest to the participant's father's birthday. Remind the participants again of the criteria used and the feedback each person received.

Close by inviting every participant to make a statement, in the table groups, about his or her understanding of his or her call to ministry. Then invite everyone to sing or read the text of "Lord God, Your Love Has Called Us Here" (*Hymnal*, 579). (If this tune is unfamiliar, it may also be sung to the more familiar tune "Faith of Our Fathers.") Finally, read together "The Apostolic Blessing" (*Hymnal*, 669).

Session Five:
Called to Grow in Faith

The main purposes of this session are

- to provide a laboratory preaching experience through preparing, presenting, and receiving feedback;
- to understand that being a Christian, and especially being a lay speaker in The United Methodist Church, is both grounded and propelled by a personal and growing faith in Jesus Christ as Lord and Savior;
- to recognize the importance of spiritual discipline for a growing faith.

Supplies and resources
- *The United Methodist Hymnal*
- *Lay Speaking Ministries: Basic Course*
- Bibles
- Bible concordances and other Bible study aids
- Newsprint
- Felt-tip markers
- Masking tape
- Participant journals
- Pens or pencils

Outline

Part 1: Called to proclaim the gospel through growing in personal faith
1. Welcome and reading (4 minutes)
2. Preaching experiences (30 minutes)
3. Reflection (5 minutes)
4. Ways to commune with God (13 minutes)
5. Prayer and reflection (10 minutes)

STRETCH BREAK (5 minutes)

Part 2: Closing
6. Bible study (25 minutes)
7. Identifying role models (8 minutes)
8. Examining lifestyles (7 minutes)
9. Reflection (8 minutes)
10. Covenant and commissioning (12 minutes)

TOTAL TIME: 2 hours, 7 minutes

SESSION PLAN

1. Welcome group members by name and read responsively, as a prayer, Psalm 5 (*The United Methodist Hymnal*, 742–43).

2. Divide the participants into new groups of three to present their mini-sermons. Once again, remind everyone of the criteria you have used in each session and of the need to give helpful feedback and encouragement. Keep time carefully.

   When the groups have nearly finished, ask them to discuss how preparing a traditional fifteen- to twenty-minute message will differ from the assignments they have had.

3. Direct everyone to spend time personally reflecting on the experience of speaking and the comments they received. Ask them to write about those feelings and insights in their journals and to reflect on the question "What is God's message to me?"

4. Remind the participants that a growing faith requires discipline: discipline in our time and habits; discipline to worship God. We are called to commune with God in every waking and sleeping moment, to make every thought and deed a prayer.

   Ask the participants to discuss, in table groups, how they would respond if a new believer asked them how to commune with God. Then direct the participants, in groups of three, to tell their most significant and most difficult experiences of communing with God.

5. Encourage the participants to sit in a comfortable position and to turn to "Lead Me, Lord" (*Hymnal*, 473). Ask the participants to pray, silently and repeatedly, the phrase "Lead me, Lord, lead me in thy righteousness; make thy way plain before my face" as a breath prayer (described in Chapter 9 in this manual). Allow up to seven full minutes for this experience. (It will seem like an eternity.) Then ask the participants to form pairs and reflect with one another on the experience.

STRETCH BREAK

6. Remind the participants of the phrase "Walk the talk" described in Chapter 10. Assign table groups one of these stories: Ananias and Sapphira (Acts 4:32–5:11), Uriah (2 Samuel 11:1-13), or Zacchaeus (Luke 19:1-9). Have the groups read their assigned story, considering these questions:

- What was at issue?
- How did the character respond?
- In what way did (or did not) she or he walk the talk?

Then direct each table group to represent creatively (possibly through drama, interview, or music) their character and incident to the rest of the group.

7. Ask the participants to identify a person or people who exemplify Christian witness; that is, whose personal lifestyle clearly demonstrates the Christian faith. Recall specific examples of how the faith is lived. Have each participant discuss his or her insights with one other group member.

8. This manual describes several facets of any lifestyle for consideration by the Christian: values, prejudices, priorities, approaches to life, and social stances, to name a few. Direct the table groups to discuss and define a Christian lifestyle (recognizing that this term has become politicized in recent years).

9. Have all the participants spend time in personal assessment, asking, *How well do I walk the talk? What can I do in the next week to better walk the talk for Jesus Christ?* Encourage the participants to actually write a plan for the next week.

10. "A Covenant Prayer in the Wesleyan Tradition" (*Hymnal,* 607) is a meaningful prayer for the Christian disciple. Ask individuals to read the prayer silently. Emphasize the seriousness of these words. Then, with an invitation to make this commitment, invite all to read this prayer together.

Invite the table groups to join hands and pray for the ministry of each participant in the coming months.

End the training event by singing or speaking confidently the lyrics to "Lord, You Give the Great Commission" (*Hymnal,* 584).

Additional Resources

Forbid Them Not: Involving Children in Sunday Worship (3 volumes: Year A, Year B, Year C), by Carolyn C. Brown (Abingdon Press, 1992, 1993, 1994), is a lectionary-based series that includes helps for children's messages and sermon starters.

A Guide to Prayer for All God's People, by Rueben P. Job and Norman Shawchuck (Upper Room Books, reprint 1990), is a great resource for the practice of daily disciplines and for personal retreats.

Prayers for the Seasons of God's People: Worship Aids for the Revised Common Lectionary (3 volumes: Year A, Year B, Year C), by B. David Hostetter (Abingdon Press, 1997, 1998, 1999).

Teaching the Bible to Adults and Youth, by Dick Murray (Abingdon Press, 1993), contains practical helps for teaching the Bible.

What Every Leader Needs to Know (Discipleship Resources, 2004). This series of booklets includes help on the topics of leading in a congregation, leading meetings, leading prayer, purpose, and United Methodist connections.

What Every Teacher Needs to Know (Discipleship Resources, 2002). This series of booklets can help when you are called upon to teach a class. The topics covered are the Bible, Christian heritage, the classroom environment, curriculum, faith language, living the faith, people, teaching, theology, and The United Methodist Church.

The Upper Room Disciplines (Upper Room Books, yearly) is an excellent resource for personal spiritual growth.

The Book of Discipline of The United Methodist Church— 2004 (The United Methodist Publishing House, 2004) is the book of law of The United Methodist Church.

The Faith We Sing (The United Methodist Publishing House, 2000) offers hymns reflecting a range of worship styles and cultural backgrounds.

The United Methodist Book of Worship (The United Methodist Publishing House, 1992) contains a wide variety of material to assist in planning worship.

The United Methodist Hymnal (The United Methodist Publishing House, 1989) includes a wide variety of resources for worship planning.

The United Methodist *Discipline* Regarding Lay Speakers

Conference Role

¶ 629. *Conference Board of Discipleship*—The annual conference shall organize a **board of discipleship** or other *equivalent* structure to provide for these functions and maintain the connectional relationship between the General Board of Discipleship and the conference, district, and local church, and to provide for discipleship functions related to the objectives and scope of work of the General Board of Discipleship as set forth in ¶¶ 1101, 1102. The person or persons serving as member(s) of the General Board of Discipleship shall be member(s) of the conference board of discipleship and may be granted voting privileges.

1. *General Responsibilities*— . . . *i)* To determine the necessary directors, coordinators, or designated leaders for discipleship responsibilities at the annual conference level, including the maintenance of linkage with the General Board of Discipleship and related district committees within the annual conference.

¶ 630. *Conference Board of Laity*—1. There shall be in every annual conference a **conference board of laity** or other equivalent structure to provide for these functions and maintain connectional relationship. It shall provide for the ministry of the laity related to the objectives of the General Board of Discipleship as set forth in ¶¶ 1101–1127.

2. The purpose of the conference board of laity shall be: . . .

e) To provide organization, direction, and support for the development of local church leaders. . . .

7. *Responsibilities in the area of Ministry of the Laity—a)* To develop and promote programs to cultivate an adequate understanding of the theological and biblical basis for ministry of the laity among the members of the churches of the annual conference; to give special emphasis to programs and services that will enable laity of all ages to serve more effectively as leaders in both church and community. . . .

d) To organize a conference committee on Lay Speaking Ministries that will fulfill the requirements of ¶¶ 267–269 on behalf of the conference. This committee shall set guidelines and criteria to be used by district committees (*see* ¶ 665).

District Role

¶ 665. *District Committee on Lay Speaking Ministries*—Districts are encouraged to create a **district committee on Lay Speaking Ministries** related to the annual conference through the conference committee on Lay Speaking Ministries.

1. The purpose of the district committee on Lay Speaking Ministries is to plan and supervise the program within the district.

2. The committee is chaired by the district director of Lay Speaking Ministries. In addition to the director, membership of the committee will include the district lay leader, the district superintendent, and an instructor of lay speaking courses. Other resource people may be added as needed.

3. The responsibilities of a district committee on Lay Speaking Ministries are to provide basic training for local church lay speakers and advanced courses for certified lay speakers as recommended by the General Board of Discipleship, or as approved by the conference committee on Lay Speaking Ministries; to decide who will be recognized as certified lay speakers; to help match lay speakers . . . with service opportunities; and to support and affirm lay speakers . . . as they serve.

4. The district committee shall plan advanced courses for lay speaking that will enable certified lay speakers to maintain that recognition.

5. The district committee will report to the pastor and charge conference of each certified lay speaker the courses that have been satisfactorily completed by the certified lay speaker.

Lay Speaking Ministries

¶ 267. *Lay Speaking*—1. A **lay speaker** (local church or certified) is a professing member of a local church or charge who is ready and desirous to serve the Church and who is well informed on and committed to the Scriptures and the doctrine, heritage, organization, and life of The United Methodist Church and who has received specific training to develop skills in witnessing to the Christian faith through spoken communication, church and community leadership, and care-giving ministries. An applicant must be active in the support of the local church or charge.

2. Lay speakers are to serve the local church or charge (or beyond the local church or charge) in any way in which their witness or leadership and service inspires the laity to deeper commitment to Christ and more effective discipleship, including the interpretation of the Scriptures, doctrine, organization, and ministries of the church.

3. Through continued study and training a lay speaker should prepare to undertake one or more of the following functions, giving primary attention to service within the local church or charge.

a) To take initiative in giving leadership, assistance, and support to the program emphases of the church.

b) To lead meetings for prayer, training, study, and discussion when requested by the pastor, district superintendent, or committee on lay speaking.

c) To conduct, or assist in conducting, services of worship, and present sermons and addresses when requested by the pastor, district superintendent, or committee on lay speaking.

d) To relate to appropriate committees and ministry areas in providing leadership for congregational and community life and fostering care-giving ministries.

4. Lay speaker training courses shall be those recommended by the General Board of Discipleship or alternates approved by the conference committee on lay speaking. Such training should enable ministries with all language and cultural groups as appropriate.

5. It is recommended that a service of commitment be held for persons recognized as local church or certified lay speakers.

¶ 268. *Local Church Lay Speaker*—1. A candidate may be recognized as a local church lay speaker by the district or conference committee on lay speaking after the candidate has:

a) Made application in writing to the appropriate committee and has been recommended by the pastor and the church council or the charge conference of the local church in which membership is held. The district superintendent shall be responsible for reporting the names of applicants to the appropriate committee.

b) Completed the basic course for lay speaking.

2. The local church lay speaker shall serve the local church in which membership is held by witness of the spoken word, vital leadership service, and care-giving ministry (see ¶ 267.3).

3. To maintain status, a report and reapplication with recommendations must be submitted annually and a refresher course approved by the Conference Committee on Lay Speaking Ministries must be completed once in every three years (*see* ¶ 247.11).

¶ 269. *Certified Lay Speaker*—1. A candidate may be recognized as a certified lay speaker by the district or conference committee on Lay Speaking Ministries after the candidate has:

a) Made application in writing to the appropriate committee and has been recommended by the pastor and the church council or the charge conference of the local church in which he or she holds membership.

b) Completed both basic and one advanced training courses for lay speaking.

c) Had his or her qualifications reviewed and approved by the appropriate committee (see ¶ 259.2 *f* [9]).

2. The certified lay speaker shall continue to serve the local church in the witness of the spoken word, vital leadership service, and care-giving ministry (see ¶ 267.1). In addition, the certified lay speaker may serve in the district and conference and in local churches other than the local church in which membership is held.

3. Recognition as a certified lay speaker shall be renewed annually by the district or conference committee on Lay Speaking Ministries after the certified lay speaker has:

a) Requested in writing the renewal of certification.

b) Submitted an annual report to the charge conference and the committee on Lay Speaking Ministries, giving evidence of the satisfactory performance of lay speaking service.

c) Been recommended for renewal by the pastor and the church council or charge conference.

d) Completed at least once in every three years an advanced course for lay speakers.

¶ 270. *Transfer of Certification by Certified Lay Speakers*—A certified lay speaker who moves may transfer certification to the new district upon receipt of a letter from the previous district's committee on Lay Speaking Ministries confirming current certification and the date of completion of the most recent advanced course taken. Further renewal of certification is in accordance with ¶ 269.